Heritage Studies in the Muslim World

Series Editor
Trinidad Rico
Rutgers University
New Brunswick
New Jersey, USA

"Heritage" is implicated in the creation and circulation of categories through which Islam is studied and understood. The categories used in the management, identification, and safeguarding efforts of all heritage—authenticity, integrity, endangerment, values, and stewardship—are built on relationships between communities and their history, identity, politics, and beliefs, which are often employed as categories and relationships that are rigorous and normative. In contrast, a critical heritage framework recognizes the diversity of heritage constructs across territories and time and, accordingly, aims to destabilize these categories by considering and revealing the agendas and biases that have nurtured these categories and their underlying relationships, methodological approaches, and research agendas.

The series *Heritage Studies in the Muslim World* invites a breakaway from disciplinary legacies that are involved in the study of "Islamic heritage." It features broad representation of disciplines and voices that intersect at this subject of study, with scholarship that is often located at the margins of disciplines and domains. In this aim, the series welcomes a broad representation of voices that intersect to address heritage discourses and practices, considering the natural and built environment, material culture, traditions, performances, technologies, discourses, and other political and legal instruments that are associated with heritage. Contributors to this series recognize the Muslim world as a diverse and fluid territory where Muslim and non-Muslim communities engage with Muslim and non-Muslim heritage constructs.

More information about this series at
http://www.springer.com/series/15128

Trinidad Rico
Editor

The Making of Islamic Heritage

Muslim Pasts and Heritage Presents

Editor
Trinidad Rico
Rutgers University
New Brunswick, New Jersey, USA

Heritage Studies in the Muslim World
ISBN 978-981-10-4070-2   ISBN 978-981-10-4071-9 (eBook)
DOI 10.1007/978-981-10-4071-9

Library of Congress Control Number: 2017937891

© The Editor(s) (if applicable) and The Author(s) 2017. This book is an open access publication.

Open Access   This book is licensed under the terms of the Creative Commons Attribution 4.0 International License (http://creativecommons.org/licenses/by/4.0/), which permits use, sharing, adaptation, distribution and reproduction in any medium or format, as long as you give appropriate credit to the original author(s) and the source, provide a link to the Creative Commons license and indicate if changes were made.

The images or other third party material in this book are included in the book's Creative Commons license, unless indicated otherwise in a credit line to the material. If material is not included in the book's Creative Commons license and your intended use is not permitted by statutory regulation or exceeds the permitted use, you will need to obtain permission directly from the copyright holder.

The use of general descriptive names, registered names, trademarks, service marks, etc. in this publication does not imply, even in the absence of a specific statement, that such names are exempt from the relevant protective laws and regulations and therefore free for general use.

The publisher, the authors and the editors are safe to assume that the advice and information in this book are believed to be true and accurate at the date of publication. Neither the publisher nor the authors or the editors give a warranty, express or implied, with respect to the material contained herein or for any errors or omissions that may have been made. The publisher remains neutral with regard to jurisdictional claims in published maps and institutional affiliations.

Cover image: Pattern adapted from an Indian cotton print produced in the 19th century

Printed on acid-free paper

This Palgrave Macmillan imprint is published by Springer Nature
The registered company is Springer Nature Singapore Pte Ltd.
The registered company address is: 152 Beach Road, #21-01/04 Gateway East, Singapore 189721, Singapore

Acknowledgments

This edited book is the result of two academic events that I hosted in Doha between 2014 and 2016 in order to explore the way that different disciplinary interventions *create* a field subject of "Islamic heritage" through their specific methodologies: the first event was a research workshop titled "Islamic Pasts," held in December 2014 at UCL Qatar; and the second was a conference session titled "Islamic Presents," which was part of the Liberal Arts International Conference organized in January 2016 at Texas A&M University at Qatar. Following these focused initiatives, the completion of this edited book relied, above all, on the support, patience, and feedback from the contributors themselves, and I would therefore like to thank them again for investing their time and scholarship on this small collection. In addition, I would like to thank the blind peer reviewers for their critical but encouraging comments on earlier versions of this book, and Dr. Giulia El Dardiry and Dr. Imad Mansour for their logistical support, their generous thoughts, and their endless supply of *mana'eesh* and *tabouleh* during our shared time as scholars in Doha.

This book was made possible by a Conference and Workshop Sponsorship Program grant from the Qatar National Research Fund (a member of Qatar Foundation).

Contents

1 The Making of Islamic Heritages: An Overview of Disciplinary Interventions   1
Trinidad Rico

2 The Intertwining of History and Heritage in Islamic Contexts   13
Shahzad Bashir

3 Muslim Cultures and Pre-Islamic Pasts: Changing Perceptions of "Heritage"   23
R. Michael Feener

4 Reclaiming Heritage Through the Image of Traditional Habitat   47
Ali Mozaffari and Nigel Westbrook

5 Framing the Primordial: Islamic Heritage and Saudi Arabia   67
Ömer Can Aksoy

6 Images of Piety or Power? Conserving the Umayyad Royal Narrative in Qusayr ʿAmra   91
Gaetano Palumbo

7 The Buddha Remains: Heritage Transactions in Taxila, Pakistan 109
   Hassan Asif and Trinidad Rico

Index 125

List of Figures

Fig. 4.1	A pedestrian walkway in Shushtar No'w, development stage 1	56
Fig. 4.2	General view of Shushtar No'w rooftops, development stage 1	58
Fig. 6.1	Two of the "kings" before and after conservation. The 1975 intervention did not allow the perception of the "real" quality of the paintings	95
Fig. 6.2	One of the numerous representations of Prophet Jonah found in Qusayr 'Amra	97
Fig. 6.3	Standing figure holding a basket of grapes, flanked by a feline (a panther?)—perhaps a representation of Dionysus	99
Fig. 6.4	The so-called Six Kings panel, either representing the kings defeated by the Umayyads, the six regions of the Earth, or the recipients of Prophet Mohammad's embassies	100
Fig. 7.1	Buddhist relic caskets placed in front of Islamic calligraphy with "Allah" inscribed on the stone (left); schist stone lying by the gate of Raheem's house (center); Buddha sculpture in the *bodhisattva* stage, unveiled from behind a plant pot (right)	111

CHAPTER 1

The Making of Islamic Heritages: An Overview of Disciplinary Interventions

Trinidad Rico

Abstract This chapter introduces the challenge that brought together the contributors to this collection of essays, describing the trajectory that heritage studies has had in the face of established discourses about Islam and heritage in order to suggest ways in which these perceptions can be disrupted. In this introductory chapter, I define the value of involving different disciplinary conversations and forms of expertise that entangle specific languages, boundaries, categories, and concerns in the shaping of "Islamic heritage" as a subject of study. I propose that a consideration of alternative modes of thinking and established biases may be an essential tool to rupture the current problematic trajectory in critical heritage work about Muslim communities and their construction of heritage value.

Keywords Expertise · interdisciplinarity · critical heritage

Making Heritages

In a space of definitional ambiguity and through an appeal to inclusivity, both Islam and heritage have been said to be "all things to all people" (Ahmed 1998, xi; Larkham 1995, 85). In consideration of this

T. Rico (✉)
Rutgers University, New Brunswick, New Jersey, USA

© The Author(s) 2017
T. Rico (ed.), *The Making of Islamic Heritage*, Heritage Studies in the Muslim World, DOI 10.1007/978-981-10-4071-9_1

simultaneously privileged and inconvenient proposition, this collection of chapters takes the intersection of these complex concepts—Islamic heritage—as a challenging site of construction, where different viewpoints, in the form of disciplines, their sources and methods of analysis, shape both a subject of study and a process of heritage recognition. This collection does not aim to promote the existence of a discrete category of "Islamic heritage" or characterize or authorize what is "Islamic" about this construct; contributors do acknowledge, however, that Islamic heritage as a category is often constructed and circulated as a discrete, identifiable designation. Therefore, these chapters are not addressing heritage from a teleological position—they neither prescribe how to maintain or define a relationship between religious, sacred, and secular values in the work of tangible and intangible heritage in Muslim contexts,[1] nor do they aim to promote or endorse any specific iteration of Islamic heritage.[2] Rather than doing this type of definitional work, this concise collection of essays takes a processual approach, considering practices of designating (or erasing) value that can be conceptualized—but may not be explicitly referred to—as "heritage" in the context of Islam and the disciplinary viewpoints that mediate these processes.

This emphasis is motivated by a positional challenge that is core to advances in critical heritage studies. On the one hand, it considers whether practices for heritage preservation in Muslim contexts can be productively discussed in opposition to (Western) dominant heritage practices (or AHD, see Smith 2006); and on the other hand, it remains considerate of the imposition of reductionist conceptual orthodoxies that are embedded in the very notion of "heritage" and what is expected of heritage practices. Therefore, the focus of the chapters in this collection lies on the way that different disciplines facilitate specific heritage debates as they navigate the concept of Islamic heritage through their particular methodologies, sources, languages, and boundaries. In doing so, each disciplinary viewpoint enables specific genres of stakeholders that may be instrumental to understanding the construction of Islamic heritage in the present and in the past.[3] The inclusion of nondisciplinary stakeholders in particular has been central to the development of critical heritage approaches worldwide, which promote inclusivity of subaltern voices as a way toward decentralization of authority and a pluralization of heritage histories and methods (see, for example, Meskell 2011; Shackel 2009; Shepherd 2002). However, considering a form of agency that cannot be dissociated from disciplinary constructions of heritage but which remains largely un-problematized

(Rico 2017), I have encouraged contributors to suspend momentarily an emphasis on the prioritization of stakeholders and their voices. I asked them instead to tackle reflexively the ways in which their discipline constructs and promotes instruments and platforms for the inclusion of plural "Islamic heritages," relying on assumptions about the way that the past and the present are mediated. In so doing, these chapters contribute to our understanding of the way that heritage is implicated in the work of "othering" (Butler 2006, 463), differentiating, and ordering populations (Bennett 2006; Bennett et al. 2017).

The subtitle of this edited collection, *Muslim Pasts and Heritage Presents*, presents an intentional asymmetry in terms, hinting at the diverse and nonlinear ways in which the past and the present are made to connect through constructions of Islamic heritage. Whereas there have been plenty of definitions proposed for heritage, the centrality of the present in its process of construction makes heritage best understood and managed as "a contemporary product shaped from history" (Turnbridge and Ashworth 1996, 20). However, the nature of the "present-centeredness" of heritage is not thoroughly addressed by the discipline of heritage studies (Harvey 2001, 3), enabling the circulation of established thematic restrictions and temporal biases in the construction of disciplinary histories—undiscerningly and against the objectives of a critical turn for the discipline. In his article "Heritage Pasts and Heritage Presents," David Harvey (2001) argues that heritage has always been produced and consumed in contextually appropriate ways. He questions the persistence of a surprisingly linear history of heritage—or "heritage of heritage"—and argues that it is the product of restricted geographical and temporal information with an uncontested point of origin in nineteenth-century Europe. Furthermore, he contends that there has been little effort to pluralize heritage practices in consideration of shifting presents that should result in extremely diverse heritage histories (Harvey 2001, 6). Therefore, a consideration of the restrictions brought about by disciplinary modes of seeing brings them to the foreground for further examination. In this book, we begin the dual work of charting additional geographical and temporal engagements in the improvement of disciplinary histories of critical heritage studies and of mapping Islamic heritages as active constructs that are negotiated in specific contexts and beyond the dominance of present-day themes of conflict and destruction (Rico 2014).

With this temporally dynamic focus in mind, this volume brings together different disciplinary vantage points and considerations on the construction of Islamic heritage as a subject of study. This effort considers, for example, the way that a predominantly visual appraisal of heritage value relies on and does definitional work through aesthetics, resulting in a heritage resource that is documented predominantly, if not exclusively, through its aesthetic value. Likewise, a historical appraisal of heritage leads to the creation of a heritage construct that is defined extensively through its historicity, and so on. Overlooked possibilities of inquiry include an examination of the circumstances under which construction, destruction, and mobilization of heritage value in Muslim contexts and sources occur as well as the channels of authority and expertise that are deployed in these processes. Different disciplinary engagements with Islamic heritage reiterate and authorize established patterns and themes of discussion—informing and appealing to concerned heritage audiences internationally at a time of widespread tensions between Muslim and non-Muslim communities and state actors worldwide.

Therefore, the work of critically reappraising Islamic heritage in this volume considers not only *what* the construct of Islamic heritage authorizes and perpetuates but also what different disciplines that contribute to heritage studies *allow* Islamic heritage to authorize and perpetuate through their practices, values, and standards. The chapters in this volume confront many of the preconceptions involved in addressing Islamic heritage as a construct that foregrounds heritage as a material and monolithic category—an indicator of the powerful dominance of notions attached to "heritage." This materialist construction of Islamic heritage is the subject of a number of misconceptions that have persisted over time and that have had significant influence on disciplinary approaches to this type of material culture from within the heritage industry, including: that historical Islamic narratives must be understood from a past-centered perspective; that Islamic heritage serves an Islamic past; and that Islamic values are static and perceptible (see Bashir 2014). When considered as an overlapping set of truth claims, these preconceptions help us to understand the fleeting nature of any definition of Islamic heritages as an analytical construct that should be addressed in the context of changing contemporary notions of Muslim material culture. With this problematic in mind, contributors face the challenge of exploring how disciplinary interventions effectively create Islamic heritages, with the aim of addressing—or rather, redressing—the place of Islamic heritage within their own disciplinary practices and in order to redirect discussions of this topic in more varied and constructive directions.

Disciplinary Interventions

Attending to the most visible issue in the study of heritage as the product of disciplinary intersections, the contributors to this collection feature case studies that support significantly different constructions of heritage as a subject of study. For example, Shahzad Bashir argues through the lens of religious studies that heritage is that which is made valuable in a given context, a "valuable past" that is based on assessments of worth and which can be observed to be a factor of continuous significance in Islam. His contribution (Chapter 2) considers the production and circulation of this value in dynamic association with Islamic historical identity. He considers the diversity of relationships with the past that can be read, observed, and otherwise deduced from documented engagements with subjects of "Islamic heritage" at different times, in order to demonstrate that this process cannot be settled into a single narrative. In this work, Bashir argues that attention be paid to the constructive role of text in the creation of and attitudes toward heritage. Consequently, what is to be regarded as Islamic heritage depends fundamentally on today's understanding of the frame within which it was produced, and to this effect, he advocates that we take note of the particularities of the Islamic evidence that we encounter while remaining mindful of our own interpretive commitments.

On a related argument, R. Michael Feener's discussion (Chapter 3) offers a historical perspective that characterizes the variety of Muslim experiences with and appreciation of pre-Islamic cultural legacies as processes of making meaning in terms of Islam. Feener examines these processes through a series of historical vignettes describing medieval and early modern encounters between Muslims and the material remains of past civilizations that remained visible in the lands where they lived, ranging from Egypt to the Indonesian island of Java. Taken together, the historical data presented in this chapter compellingly demonstrate that there is no single, normative "Islamic" approach to the cultural heritage of pre-Islamic civilizations, as there are different types of engagements with and appreciations of elements of pre-Islamic pasts.

There are also different types of outcomes during the cultural encounters that contextualize these approaches. In parallel to calls for "authenticity" that are central to many preservation discourses, Feener argues that hybrid or vernacular products in the Muslim world may be subject to calls for "purification." Ali Mozaffari and Nigel Westbrook's contribution (Chapter 4) addresses such a process by examining the "model community" of Shushtar No'w in Iran. Shushtar No'w was intended to bridge the gap between Iranian culture, its heritage, and modern urbanism through the mobilization of architectural motifs and images that were used to evoke and perhaps invoke "authentic" traditional life. Mozaffari and Westbrook examine the construction of this site in the context of a twofold process that destabilizes the way in which this Islamic architectural heritage discourse is formed: on the one hand, they bring attention to the complex networks that constructed "Islamic housing" in a process that implicated colonial governing of "indigeneity" in French North Africa, and on the other hand, they consider the way in which this particular site was constructed to become an icon of Islamic heritage preservation through the designation of value by powerful forms of expertise, which had the ability to turn otherwise dissonant and vernacularized heritage constructs into authentic and exemplary forms of heritage preservation and management.

In a different example of the coexistence of dichotomous frameworks, Ömer Can Aksoy's work (Chapter 5) challenges the validity of the identifier, "Islamic," in the construction of Islamic heritage, while considering its use in institutional designations across Saudi Arabia. Considering the mastering of chronological hierarchies in Islam through archaeological and museum sources, Aksoy argues that, while Islamic heritage is used to define tangible and intangible heritage institutionally, it is simultaneously problematized through the view that all pasts can be made into Islamic pasts, beyond chronological and geographical particularities. The absence of contrast against which things can be made Islamic, he suggests, results in a peculiar situation: one in which no period of the past is framed as Islamic within the context of the Islamic world. He examines this articulation through an exploration of Saudi Arabian museums and the Hejaz Railway, both of which are presented as products of an official Wahhabi historiography and heritage management despite archaeological evidence that may suggest an emphasis on other chronologies.

Focusing on the role of conservation's intervention in the authentication of chronologies, Gaetano Palumbos's contribution (Chapter 6) considers the way in which images define the "Islamic" authority of a site. He summarizes the history of interventions in Qusayr' Amra, Jordan, as a process that simultaneously clarifies the phases of production of a site across its periods of occupation while also obscuring a disciplinary ability to clearly designate the "Islamic value" of this heritage place in the face of the uncovering of features that could be seen as "un-Islamic." While conservators and archaeologists at the site consider the potential and actual tensions involved in this palimpsest of imageries and what it means for the place of Qusayr' Amra in the formative history of "Islamic art," the relatively recent involvement of nondisciplinary stakeholders reveals that a variety of interpretations of the site are able to coexist through the ambiguous lens of Islamic heritage—a construct that extends beyond the authority of the designation "Islamic art," which is specific to disciplinary discourses. As Palumbo highlights in this chapter, this plurality may complicate the management of this heritage site for conservators and archaeologists who would benefit from a clearer articulation of value systems.

Echoing the tensions expected from the multiple and dissonant heritage values of different groups in Qusayr' Amra, the final chapter of this collection (Chapter 7) considers the widespread misconception that Muslim communities actively refuse to coexist and engage with non-Muslim heritages. Hassan Asif and I offer a discussion of the ways in which individuals and groups negotiate their engagements with Gandharan Buddhist art as a non-Islamic art form in consideration of their own faith and societal rules, and against widely circulated examples and debates on the merit of iconoclasm of Buddhist heritage in the region. This ethnographic case study demonstrates a way in which artists partake in the production of "Islamic" stone sculpture in the public realm, and "Buddhist" heritage in the private realm, while successfully negotiating the heritage value of an archaeological past, the responsibility of maintaining secrecy in their own Muslim society, and the demands of an international market for Buddhist art. Rather than conceptualizing the work of these artists in terms of redressing a widespread notion in heritage studies of dissonant or conflicting values, this chapter encourages a more nuanced understanding of the vital ways in which disciplinary modes of seeing can differ from local ways of negotiating participation in Islamic and non-Islamic heritage making.

This final chapter, in particular, draws attention to the way that disciplinary involvements may disrupt otherwise coherent ontologies within and about the production of Islamic heritage in the present. Furthermore, this discussion suggests that we should work to identify ways in which disciplinary interventions create or enhance conflicting encounters themselves, even while they claim to reveal them. To this end, the authors in this collection bring much-needed complexity to global preservation history itself, which has often simplified the encounter of Muslim subjects with non-Muslim material culture in light of contemporary geopolitics and biases. What we learn from Bashir's perspective is that overlapping and competing discourses about the past coexist, as he urges that we embrace the problematization of temporality in order to avoid reading different contexts as simple continuations of one another that cohere in a linear chronological development for Islamic attitudes toward the past. Feener's chapter demonstrates that culture contact between Muslim and non-Muslims results in interesting vernacular and cosmopolitan heritages. Mozaffari and Westbrook argue that what is discussed as vernacular and "syncretic" heritage can be nonetheless transformed into authentic forms of heritage that exist simultaneously as the product of various reactions to culture contact and as forms of resistance to forces of globalization. Aksoy's discussion highlights that the very ability of Islamic heritage to exist is negotiated contextually through a resistance to acknowledge the existence of anything outside of "Islam." We learn from Palumbo's contribution that the coexistence of a palimpsest of "Islamic" and "non-Islamic" art is not easily resolved by disciplinary interventions that rely on linearity of time and coherence of style in the search for "authenticity," but that the inclusion of diverse nondisciplinary stakeholders enables the coexistence of multiple viewpoints.

Taken together, these chapters demonstrate that a deeper examination of the texts, narratives, standards, methodologies, and modes of inquiry that are used to understand the mobilization of Islamic heritages is needed. Moreover, these discussions suggest that agents of heritage construction, which include heritage experts, scholars, and nondisciplinary stakeholders alike, problematize the ideas of "heritage values" and "Islamic values" in ingenious ways, fitting different narratives of the past to different purposes in active modes of production. Hence, it is important to understand the connections and roles involved in the examination of a material culture that is constructed to act as the heritage of Muslim communities. Rather than validating the imagination of a monolithic and temporally cohesive Islamic past, the chapters in this volume encourage an awareness of multiple forms of the pasts that are strategically utilized in the construction of heritage in multiple present contexts. Despite the diversity of case studies and approaches, the contributions collected here argue in unison that values ascribed on specific heritages across the Muslim world are associated with the ways of seeing of disciplinary frameworks, informed by social and political milieus that contextualize them and circulated as artifacts in conversation with broader disciplinary debates and sources.

Notes

1. See the critical work on issues of material religion by Morgan, "Introduction: The Matter of Belief," and Meyer and Houtman, "Introduction: How Things Matter."
2. Discussions in this volume unanimously address Islamic heritage as a temporally, spatially, and disciplinarily situated construct. As such, it would be preferably addressed within quotes, as "Islamic heritage," as a way of explicitly recognizing that the term is used as an analytical construct that should be conceptualized within discussions offered by each author. However, considering the numerous times that this term is used throughout this collection, I have taken the editorial decision to keep the term without quotes, except where authors use them to highlight specific issues they are discussing.
3. For example, see Assi, *Islamic Waqf and Management of Cultural Heritage Palestine*, for discussions of the historical construction of architectural heritage, and Peutz, *Bedouin "Abjection": World Heritage, Worldliness, and Worthiness at the Margins of Arabia*, for an ethnographic example of the significance of subaltern voices in the construction of heritage value.

Bibliography

Ahmed, Akbar S. 1998. *Islam Today: A Short Introduction to the Muslim World*. London: I.B. Tauris.

Assi, Eman. 2008. "Islamic Waqf and Management of Cultural Heritage Palestine." *International Journal of Heritage Studies* no. 14 (4): 380–385.

Bashir, Shahzad. 2014. "On Islamic Time: Rethinking Chronology in the Historiography of Muslim Societies." *History and Theory* no. 53 (4): 519–544.

Bennett, Tony. 2006. "Exhibition, Difference and the Logic of Culture." In *Museum Frictions: Public Cultures/Global Transformations*, edited by Ivan Karp and Corinne A. Kratz, 46–49. Durham, NC: Duke University Press.

Bennett, Tony, Fiona Cameron, Nélia Dias, Ben Dibley, Rodney Harrison, Ira Jacknis, and Conal McCarthy eds. forthcoming 2017. *Collecting, Ordering, Governing: Anthropology, Museums and Liberal Government*. Durham, NC: Duke University Press.

Butler, Beverly. 2006. "Heritage and the Present Past." In *Handbook of Material Culture*, edited by Christopher Tilley, Webb Keane, Susanne Kuechler, Michael Rowlands, and Patricia Spyer, 463–479. London: SAGE Publications Ltd.

Harvey, David C. 2001. "Heritage Pasts and Heritage Presents: Temporality, Meaning and the Scope of Heritage Studies." *International Journal of Heritage Studies* no. 7 (4): 319–338.

Larkham, Peter J. 1995. "Heritage as Planned and Conserved." In *Heritage, Tourism and Society*, edited by David T. Herbert, 85–116. London: Mansell.

Meskell, Lynn. 2011. *The Nature of Heritage: The New South Africa*. Malden: Wiley-Blackwell.

Meyer, Birgit, and Dick Houtman 2012. "Introduction: How Things Matter." In *Things: Religion and the Question of Materiality*, edited by Dick Houtman and Birgit Meyer, 1–26. Fordham, UK: Fordham University Press.

Morgan, David. 2009. "Introduction: The Matter of Belief." In *Religion and Material Culture*, edited by David Morgan, 1–18. New York: Routledge.

Peutz, Nathalie. 2011. "Bedouin 'Abjection': World Heritage, Worldliness, and Worthiness at the Margins of Arabia." *American Ethnologist* no. 38 (2): 338–360.

Rico, Trinidad. 2014. "Islamophobia and the Location of Heritage Debates in the Arabian Peninsula." In *Cultural Heritage in the Arabian Peninsula: Debates, Discourses and Practices*, edited by Karen Exell and Trinidad Rico, 19–32. Farnham, Surrey, UK: Ashgate.

Rico, Trinidad. 2017. "Stakeholder in Practice: 'Us,' 'Them' and the Problem of Expertise." In Archaeologies of 'Us' and 'Them': The Ethics and Politics of Indigeneity in Archaeology and Heritage, edited by Charlotta Hillerdal, Anna Karlström, and Carl-Gösta Ojala, 38–52. New York: Routledge.

Shackel, Paul A. 2009. "Foreword." In *Ethnographies and Archaeologies: Iterations of the Past*, edited by Lena Mortensen and Julie Hollowell, ix–x. Tampa: University Press of Florida.

Shepherd, Nick. 2002. "Heading South, Looking North: Why We Need a Post-Colonial Archaeology." *Archaeological Dialogues* no. 9 (2): 74–82.

Smith, Laurajane. 2006. *Uses of Heritage*. Abingdon and New York: Routledge.

Turnbridge, J.E., and G.J. Ashworth 1996. *Dissonant Heritage: The Management of the Past as a Resource in Conflict*. Chichester, UK: John Wiley & Sons.

Trinidad Rico is assistant professor and director of the Cultural Heritage and Preservation Studies program at Rutgers University, USA. Her work focuses on ethnographic heritage studies, risk and disaster, cosmopolitanism, and expertise with particular emphasis on the broader Muslim world. She is founding editor of the Pivot series *Heritage Studies in the Muslim World* (Palgrave Macmillan).

Open Access   This book is licensed under the terms of the Creative Commons Attribution 4.0 International License (http://creativecommons.org/licenses/by/4.0/), which permits use, sharing, adaptation, distribution and reproduction in any medium or format, as long as you give appropriate credit to the original author(s) and the source, provide a link to the Creative Commons license and indicate if changes were made.

The images or other third party material in this chapter are included in the chapter's Creative Commons license, unless indicated otherwise in a credit line to the material. If material is not included in the chapter's Creative Commons license and your intended use is not permitted by statutory regulation or exceeds the permitted use, you will need to obtain permission directly from the copyright holder.

CHAPTER 2

The Intertwining of History and Heritage in Islamic Contexts

Shahzad Bashir

Abstract This chapter argues that Islamic history should be imagined as an ever-expanding web of overlapping and competing discourses about the past. Islam's transhistorical presence is an illusion that is borne of the historiographical process. Clusters of evidence we can identify pertaining to Islam are traceable to moments with their own distinctive senses of past, present, and future. Consequently, what is to be regarded as Islamic heritage depends fundamentally on the frame within which it was produced. Moreover, scholarly appreciation of heritage is itself a value-laden enterprise that participates in the creation of Islamic meanings. I advocate that we pay utmost attention to the particularities of the Islamic evidence we encounter, while simultaneously avoiding reification and being mindful of our own interpretive commitments.

Keywords Islamic history · historiography · Iran · Isfahan

During a journey for the hajj from his home in northwestern Iran, the poet Afzal al-Din Khaqani (d. ca. 1186–1199) is said to have made a stop at Mada'in (Greek: Ctesiphon), the ruined capital of the pre-Islamic Sasanian

S. Bashir (✉)
Brown University, Providence, RI, USA

dynasty. The visit is said to have inspired him to write a celebrated ode (*qasida*) that begins as follows:

> Beware, O heart that sees portents, look with insight,
> consider Mada'in's great arch the admonishing mirror.
> Leaving the banks of the Tigris, alight at Mada'in,
> on its ground let spill from your eyes, another Tigris (Khaqani 1996, 162).

These verses encapsulate a relationship between past evidence and present concern that is central to discourses about heritage. Khaqani commences by commanding the listener to look at the old palace's arch, a monumental structure that still stands and is emblematic of the glories of ancient Persian empires (Bruno 1966). By the poet's guidance, the visual observation turns the ruined arch into an omen. The remains, crumbling yet magnificent, come to stand for the ravages of time. Having seen, the eye turns to a different function, shedding tears in imitation of the flow of the nearby river Tigris that once allowed Mada'in to be a thriving inhabitation. Goaded by the evidence of the dead concretized in the arch, the observing person's actions and emotions attend to mortality and other existential issues pertaining to human life.[1]

Khaqani's poetic musing on the Sasanian arch is the product of a bygone era's moral sensibilities and literary conventions. But his command to consider the pedagogical potential of traces of past lives has much in common with publicity materials produced by modern caretakers of archeological sites and museums. Signage, brochures, and guided tours at such locations invite visitors to observe old objects and imagine lives associated with them before they were removed from ordinary usage. In a larger frame, societal investment in preserving traces of certain pasts connects to intellectual and sociopolitical interests of those endowed with resources. Expressions such as that of Khaqani can be found in many, if not all, sociohistorical contexts. There is, then, something universal about cycling through past material to ruminate on the present. But what is to be considered valuable in this regard—what preserved or displayed and what destroyed or hidden—varies greatly between situations. The past is manufactured by linking evidence and contextualization, both elements being open to interpretation and manipulation.

The question of heritage—which I define as the past that is deemed valuable in a given situation—has been woven into discussions of Islam since the religion's inception. Details of the life of the Prophet

Muhammad are central to Islamic discourses about practice as well as thought, and the history of Islam's origins has been a contested field from the earliest recorded discussions. This issue extends to former and later periods too since Islamic self-understandings include, first, pre-Islamic biblical and other Near Eastern narratives about the past, and second, historical contingencies of events occurring in many regions between the sixth-century CE and the present. Disagreement over facts and interpretations has been endemic to all historical conclusions made with respect to Islam. All this diversity notwithstanding, modern academic representations have, up to our own present, tended to flatten the matter into a single timeline that runs from Muhammad to now (Bashir 2014).

For purposes of heritage studies, I suggest that Islamic history is best imagined as a dynamic process rather than a settled narrative. I recommend this on the basis of textual materials, an abundant and influential resource for thinking about Islam as a historical phenomenon. Islamic texts that pertain to history signify in double: They are elements within material culture in the same sense as buildings and archeological sites, and they contain discourses pertaining to the lives and thoughts of Muslims that have the past as a major component. The first element relates to paleography and related fields, a domain that lies beyond my current discussion. I am concerned with narrative representation of past time as a key ingredient within textual production pertaining to Islam. I believe this to be an arena marked by variety and continual evolution rather than constancy. In the manner of Khaqani urging his listener to look and be moved by the arch of Mada'in, Islamic discourses engage evidence from pasts to create meanings in presents. What things deserve observation, and what lessons one is to draw from these, can vary radically between different Islamic contexts. A historicizing look at textual representations of the past provides us resources to consider material culture in all its complexity.

Islam's Multiple Pasts

In customary modern academic practice, representations of the past that invoke Islamic themes are assessed by judging their plausibility in terms that make sense to us. Could an event have occurred as it is described, given corroborating or contradictory evidence? Are the details a logical possibility given our understanding of causality? For example, we can take the report about a person's date of death to be a fact while a miracle in which God is said to have intervened on the side of one party is likely to be discounted as rhetoric or religious belief. Through such judgments, we cull information from Islamic sources to create historiographical narratives that are viable in our own context. This approach, endemic to the modern academic field of Islamic history, has the drawback that it renders most of the contents of the original sources meaningless. These works simply do not share fully in the realist and literary conventions we take for granted. Moreover, reading in this way absolves us from reflecting on our own unstated presumptions about the past.

Counter to the existing dominant paradigm, I believe we should regard Islamic narratives about the past as rhetorical exercises that suture received information to the concerns of the present times in which they were produced. This is to say that we begin by acknowledging that writings in genres that pertain to the past (chronicles, hagiography, prosopography, etc.) depend on internal rules about evidence and are not to be treated as fiction. However, such works amalgamate information and interpretation to the point of inseparability. Rather than making ad hoc judgments about what is possible and what false, we should regard the narratives in the manner of looking at a building. The words and concepts that constitute them are like common construction materials, but the forms in which we find them are distinctive instantiations that reflect the world of the people who undertook their creation.

What we make of "Islam" holds a particularly important place when considering descriptions of the past in this way. Islam represents a commonality between narratives originating in different contexts as, for instance, we can pick one author from the ninth century and another from the nineteenth and observe that both refer to Islam as a cornerstone of their understandings of heritage, the valuable past. The usual way to interpret this commonality would be that the two authors are talking about the same phenomenon. Islam then comes to be understood as a suprahistorical entity that stands apart from the authors and is a universal reference point for both of them. This view makes excellent sense from the perspective of religious thought since it ratifies the sense of continuity that is necessary for the self-understanding of a tradition. But such an interpretation is historiographically problematic and needs a thorough reversal. I believe it is more appropriate to think that the putative two authors are "creating" Islam and are referring to quite different phenomena even as they use the same word. Historically speaking, Islam is an aspect of imagination and cannot exist beyond its particular constructions, which we know to differ greatly between different contexts. Islam's transhistorical presence is an illusion that is born of the historiographical process. In order to understand trajectories of Islamic thought, we certainly need to be cognizant of the fact that many people invoke Islam as a universal. But when working in a historicist mode, it is problematic to take the claim of continuity on face value.

The view I am proposing necessitates that we regard the history of Islam as a story riven with fissures and fractures rather than smooth chronological development along an arc that can be plotted. To take this route has repercussions for multiple aspects of the consideration of temporality. It means that synchronically—that is, at any "present" moment—we must expect understandings of the past involving Islam to be contested between different options. "History" in this instance would have to include the story of these contestations rather than a conglomeration of facts that can be established outside the frames of the narratives we possess. Furthermore, the options we may be able to identify as possibilities at a given moment must be presumed to have diachronic dimensions, indicating evolution of strands of thought in conjunction with sociohistorical contingencies. Yet further, we have to allow for the fact that entirely new interpretations can come into being and that neither the synchronic nor the diachronic aspect of this picture is predetermined according to pre-given patterns of rise and fall, unification and dispersion, and so on. All these matters are contingent on the details of the circumstances in which they are said to have occurred and become subject to narrative description. As I intend to discuss extensively in forthcoming work, this picture suggests that Islamic history should be understood as internally diverse and open to new possibilities without limits.

Outcomes

Understanding Islamic history as an open process has significant implications for considering the question of heritage. To begin, it indicates an investment away from Islamic universality. If there is no single Islamic history, then it follows that there can be no Islam that is available for transhistorical description. Instead, Islam is a conglomeration of thought and practice that is always under construction through the mediation of local factors. I believe it is important not to interpret this situation as implying a plurality of Islams. Thinking in terms of multiples rather than a singular Islam lets persist the problem of considering Islam a definable whole that stands apart from messy historical processes. It just makes room for multiple wholes rather than a single authoritative version. We need to reconsider the very nature of Islam as an object of discourse and understanding. From a historicizing perspective, Islam is best understood as a pluriform, entangled web, a singular that is irreducible to universal generalization in any dimension and needs unpacking according to analytical requirements of particular paradigms. I am suggesting that we retain Islam's nominal singularity while freeing it to signify in multiple, without any predetermined bounds. Whenever Islam is invoked as a term of intellectual and sociopolitical power, by proponents as well as opponents, it is in the singular rather than in multiples. But sociohistorical contextual observation tells us that this single Islam can refer to an extreme variety of things. On the side of "meaning," then, Islam is open-ended and ought to depend entirely on what we are able to observe relating to it in the world.

The perspective I am advocating is best explained through an example pertaining to heritage. Here I would like to concentrate on the great Friday mosque of Isfahan, Iran, which is suitable due to the great diversity of what it contains. This monument, a grand example of Islamic architecture, is also considered a repository of Iranian cultural identity and was recently designated a UNESCO World Heritage Site (UNESCO 2012). Considered synchronically as we can experience it today, the mosque is a meeting point between religious, national, and international discourses about heritage that are interdependent. From the vantage point of our historical location, the monument's status as an Islamic place of worship is inextricable from Iranian and international regimes pertaining to heritage. Visited as a tourist site by Iranians as well as foreigners in droves, it has been studied and restored most extensively by a team of Italian specialists who do not identify as Muslims (Galdieri 1972–1984). The mosque's contemporary significance as a historical repository is connected to modern national and global histories in which Islam holds particular kinds of meaning. The mosque's "heritage value" is conditioned by Islam as a "world religion," a category of modern provenance. Inasmuch as the mosque instantiates Islam, this is in a form determined by modern historiographical discourses. We go to it with expectations shaped by understandings of Islam that would have been alien to people alive centuries ago. Moreover, even today, preconceptions shaping the experience of the monument would differ greatly based on our own sociohistorical locations. The mosque is liable to have multiple modern interpretations, interlinked through the way its physicality is constituted and maintained under present regimes about the value of the type of object it is taken to be.

The meaning we can make of the mosque changes if the observer is able to "read" its various features more deeply than what meets the eye upon a tourist excursion. It turns out to be a monument remarkable for having preserved more than a 1,000 years' worth of ongoing construction and modification (Grabar 1990). The site contains a large variety of building materials and architectural styles, together with epigraphy strewn throughout its expanse. Built forms and texts found in the monument signify the many different historical moments at which the monument's material configuration continued to transform over the centuries. For example, the southern section contains two impressive domes that reflect the Seljuk dynasty's investment in Isfahan as an imperial religiopolitical center during the eleventh-century CE (Hunarfar 1956, 75–81). The chamber of Öljeitü (d. 1316) with its heavily inscribed stucco mihrab contains the date 710 AH (1310 CE) and is an effect of the Ilkhanid period. This site within the mosque reflects the public piety of a Mongol king who had recently converted to Islam (Hunarfar 1956, 116–120; Pfeiffer 1999). Extensive modifications and decoration undertaken during the Timurid period connect the mosque to Central Asia, the imperial center during the fourteenth and fifteenth centuries CE (Golombek and Wilbur 1988, 1:378–381). Additions from the Safavid period include epigraphy on a wall of the text of a public vow of repentance by the king Shah Tahmasp (d. 1576). We can read only half of this today since the bottom part broke away at some point and has not been found (Hunarfar 1956, 82).

These are some prominent examples from the trove of data pertaining to elites as well as the common people that is contained in the monument. The significant point for my purposes is that each cluster of evidence we can identify is traceable to a particular historical moment with its own sense of relevant Islamic heritage. Groups of people who inhabited the building in the eleventh century versus the fourteenth, sixteenth, or the nineteenth maintained particular imaginations of Islam and its past, present, and future. While all the evidence we see references Islam in the singular, the actual substance we can observe indicates a vast diversity of contents for the term. We can find many links between imaginations pertaining to different periods, as well as evidence for sedimentation of ideas over the course of time. But I am suggesting that we should resist reading different contexts as simple continuations of one another. Understanding the mosque as a fractured set of evidence manifests the monument as a conglomeration of interlinked items that cannot, however, be streamlined into a single story.

I believe this perspective to be truer to the nature of the development of ideas and practices pertaining to Islam. Read in this way, the mosque approximates to the trove of narrative materials pertaining to the past that has amassed over the course of more than a millennium.

The density and variety of evidence available at the site of the Friday mosque in Isfahan makes it a case exceptional for its richness. However, I would like to suggest that principles regarding Islamic pasts that I have highlighted using it as an example are applicable more generally to materials and sites large and small. The ultimate point here is that heritage is an evaluative concept and is based on assessments of worth. Not all things from the past constitute heritage in all circumstances, and the ones that do differ between times and places. When assessing evidence pertaining to Islam, I suggest that we should begin with the presumption that Islamic understandings of the past are variable, both synchronically and diachronically. Traces at our disposal indicate a tremendous variety of ways of being and acting as Muslim. The diversity of meanings on display here has been inherent in Islamic discourses for all the contexts for which we have evidence. In tandem with these facts, Islamic valuations of heritage are also fundamentally diverse and changeable. As we can see in the case of the influence of the prestige of Italian restorers and modern organizations such as UNESCO, Islamic understandings need not be seen as exclusive or hermetic. Rather, the notion of heritage itself requires historicization in all contexts, which reveals investments held by us as well as people who created earlier material forms. I believe this perspective attunes us to pay the utmost attention to the particularities of the evidence we encounter while simultaneously avoiding reification and being mindful of shadows cast by interpretive paradigms old and new. Appreciating and creating heritage are closely related, if not synonymous, matters, something that is as true today as it was for Muslims of the past whose effects we scrutinize to create our narratives.

Note

1. For a translation of the ode in full see Meisami (1996). For general information about the poet see Anna Livia Beelaert, "Kaqani Servani," *Encyclopaedia Iranica* (http://www.iranicaonline.org/articles/kaqani-ser vani). Khaqani's ode stands in a long tradition of poetic reflection on the remains of the past in Persian and Arabic. For details, see Meisami (1996), Clinton (1976), Clinton (1977), and Ali (1968–1969).

Acknowledgment This publication was made possible in part by a grant from the Carnegie Corporation of New York. The statements made and views expressed are solely the responsibility of the author.

Bibliography

Ali, Saleh Ahmad El. 1968–1969. "Al-Mada'in and Its Surrounding Area in Arabic Literary Sources." *Mesopotamia* no. 3–4: 417–39.
Bashir, Shahzad. 2014. "On Islamic Time: Rethinking Chronology in the Historiography of Muslim Societies." *History and Theory* no. 53 (4): 519–544.
Bruno, Andrea, Giorgio Gullini, and Mariangiola Cavallero. 1966. "The Preservation and Restoration of Taq-i Kisra." *Mesopotamia* no. 1 (89–108), pls. xvii–xxv, figs. 35–59.
Clinton, Jerome. 1976. "The Madaen Qasida of Xaqani Sharvani I." *Edebiyat* no. 1 (2): 153–170.
Clinton, Jerome. 1977. "The Madaen Qasida of Xaqani Sharvani II: Xaqani and al-Buhturi." *Edebiyat* no. 2 (2): 191–206.
Galdieri, Eugenio. 1972–1984. *Isfahan: Masgid-i Gum'a*. 3 vols. Rome: IsMEO.
Golombek, Lisa, and Donald Wilbur 1988. *The Timurid Architecture of Iran and Turan*. 2 vols. Vol. 1. Princeton, NJ: Princeton University Press.
Grabar, Oleg. 1990. *The Great Mosque of Isfahan*. New York: New York University Press.
Hunarfar, Lutfullah. 1956. *Ganjina-yi Asar-i Tarikhi-yi Isfahan*. Isfahan, Iran: Kitabfurushi-yi Saqafi.
Khaqani. 1996. "Elegy on Mada'in." In *Qasida Poetry in Islamic Asia and Africa: Eulogy's Bounty, Meaning's Abundance*, edited by Stefan Sperl and Christopher Shackle. Leiden, Netherlands: Brill.
Meisami, Julie Scott. 1996. "Poetic Microcosms: The Persian Qasida to the End of the Twelfth Century." In *Qasida Poetry in Islamic Asia and Africa: Classical Traditions and Modern Meanings*, edited by Stefan Sperl and Christopher Shackle, 173–182. Leiden, Netherlands: Brill.
Pfeiffer, Judith. 1999. "Conversion Versions: Sultan Öljeytü's Conversion to Shi'ism (709/1309) in Muslim Narrative Sources." *Mongolian Studies* no. 22: 35–67.
UNESCO. *Masjed-e Jāmé of Isfahan*. United Nations Educational, Scientific, and Cultural Organization (UNESCO), World Heritage Convention 2012 [accessed 25 April 2016]. Available from http://whc.unesco.org/en/list/1397.

Shahzad Bashir is Aga Khan Professor of Islamic Humanities at Brown University, USA. He specializes in intellectual and social history and is currently finishing a book entitled *Islamic Pasts and Futures: Conceptual Explorations*.

Open Access This book is licensed under the terms of the Creative Commons Attribution 4.0 International License (http://creativecommons.org/licenses/by/4.0/), which permits use, sharing, adaptation, distribution and reproduction in any medium or format, as long as you give appropriate credit to the original author(s) and the source, provide a link to the Creative Commons license and indicate if changes were made.

The images or other third party material in this chapter are included in the chapter's Creative Commons license, unless indicated otherwise in a credit line to the material. If material is not included in the chapter's Creative Commons license and your intended use is not permitted by statutory regulation or exceeds the permitted use, you will need to obtain permission directly from the copyright holder.

CHAPTER 3

Muslim Cultures and Pre-Islamic Pasts: Changing Perceptions of "Heritage"

R. Michael Feener

Abstract This chapter explores a diverse range of historic Muslim experiences with and appreciations of pre-Islamic cultural legacies. I offer an overview of Muslim interpretations of Qur'anic verses urging believers to reflect on the visible traces of pasts connected with traditions of pre-Islamic Arabia and biblical literature, followed by an examination of a series of historical vignettes relating medieval and early-modern encounters between Muslims and the material remains of past civilizations in Egypt, India, and Indonesia. These case studies clearly demonstrate that there is no single, normative "Islamic" approach to the cultural heritage of pre-Islamic civilizations. Rather, conversations about the meanings of the past for contemporary life and visions of the future are dynamic discourses incorporating an expansive body of ideas and experiences across diverse communities.

Keywords Pre-Islamic · Islamization · vernacularization · Egypt · Indonesia · India

"Have they not travelled through the land and seen how their predecessors met their end? They were mightier than them: they cultivated the

---

R.M. Feener (✉)
Oxford Centre for Islamic Studies / Faculty of History, University of Oxford, Oxford, United Kingdom

© The Author(s) 2017
T. Rico (ed.), *The Making of Islamic Heritage*, Heritage Studies in the Muslim World, DOI 10.1007/978-981-10-4071-9_3

earth more and built more upon it..." (*al-Rum*/30:9).¹ The trope of "travelling through the land" (*yasiru fi'l-ard*) to see the ruins of past civilizations occurs more than a dozen times in the Qur'an.² For over 1,400 years, as Islamic civilization spread out of Arabia and across expanding regions of Africa and Eurasia, Muslims have borne this in mind and interpreted it in diverse ways as they came into contact—and to terms— with a wide range of physical remnants of multiple pre-Islamic pasts. In interpreting these diverse monuments and ruins, recourse was often made to the meanings the Qur'an elsewhere ascribes to ancient sites in Arabia and neighboring countries. For example, in the Qur'anic *sura* (chapter) of *al-Fajr*/89:6–13, we read:

> Have you [Prophet] considered how your Lord dealt with [the people] of 'Ad of Iram [the city] of lofty pillars, whose like has never been made in any land, and the Thamud, who hewed into the rocks in the valley, and the mighty and powerful Pharaoh? All of them committed excesses in their lands, and spread corruption there: your Lord let a scourge of punishment loose on them.

Here the scope of past civilizations extends beyond Arabia to one of the most powerful symbols of antiquity in the broader region: Pharaonic Egypt. Indeed, within Muslim tradition Egypt's monumental heritage became a particularly powerful site for such reflections as that country became first a province of an expanding Muslim empire, and later a major center of Islamic learning and literature in its own right.

Egypt in Muslim Imaginations of the Pre-Islamic Past

For more than 1,000 years, Egypt has been a site for some of the most complex negotiations by Muslims with the ruins of their pre-Islamic pasts. There, diverse views and relations to this heritage have been constantly negotiated and renegotiated since the earliest period of Islamic history. For not only did Muslims encounter the remains of a lost past in the form of massive stone monuments, but the particular civilization associated with them is one that has been extensively discussed in the text of the Qur'an itself. Egypt's Pharaonic past receives considerably more attention in Islam's scripture than do the passing references to Arabian antiquities such as the pillars of 'Ad and the stonework of Thamud.

Indeed, the longest sustained narrative in the Qur'anic text is the story of Yusuf (the biblical Joseph) in *sura* 12.³ When Muslims came to Egypt and encountered the imposing ancient monuments there those ruins became indexed to the Qur'anic story in local lore and literary traditions—as with the identification of the pyramids with Yusuf's granaries, and ruins at Saqqara and in the Fayyum with the palace of Zulaykha/"Potiphar's wife" and the prison into which Yusuf was cast, respectively (Haarmann 1996). Beyond the story of Yusuf, the Qur'an also tells, evocatively and repeatedly, of Moses' (Ar. Musa) confrontation with Pharaoh. In these verses, the figure of Fira'un—and, by extension, the realm of Egypt that he ruled—represents the most extreme form of arrogant unbelief. On the one hand, the evil image of the builder of the pyramids could stir Muslim resentment and anger or even inspire works of vandalism and attempts at destroying pre-Islamic monuments. On the other hand, the Qu'anic injunctions to reflect on the ruins of ancient unbelievers could also be extended to the Pharaonic-built heritage of Egypt, thus fostering a sense of the desirability of preserving them for purposes of religious and moral pedagogy. Indeed, as Egypt's ancient ruins came to be considered among the greatest wonders (*'aja'ib*) of the world, they could also be understood by many medieval Muslims as a testament to the greatness of God's creation, as well as the power of His judgment (Haarmann 1980).

Over the course of Egypt's Islamic history, Muslims have held a range of views all along this spectrum. As Ulrich Haarman (1980, 59, 1996, 625) has demonstrated, reactions to the built heritage of the Pharaohs have included both Saladin's futile attempt to destroy the pyramids and the arguments of medieval authors such as al-Idrisi and al-Manufi in favor of a more tolerant perspective on their preservation. The motivations of those medieval Muslims who were attracted to visit the pyramids and other ruins of ancient Egypt were diverse and often went well beyond religious reflection on the vain folly of human arrogance—with the journey to see these marvels also including personal searches for both wisdom and entertainment (Haarmann 1991a). Some Muslim travelers of the Middle Ages noted their appreciation of the technical mastery required to construct works like geometrically perfect obelisks (Haarmann 1991b). Others saw the pyramids in particular as giant storehouses for buried caches of "hermetic" knowledge (Fodor 1970)⁴—with a wide range of mythic genealogies explaining the story of who it was that built the pyramids to protect this wisdom, when, and why.⁵

At the same time there were other, less esoteric, traditions associated with Pharaonic Egypt as well. Several medieval authors relate legends about and report magical powers associated with the sphinx, which accordingly was viewed by some as a source of power for cures, protection, and divination (Haarmann 1978). Despite all this, there appears to have been relatively little enthusiasm among the local ʿulamaʾ for campaigns to destroy this monument to the age of the Pharaohs. In fact, the acceptance of pre-Islamic monuments as abiding remnants of the country's past was at times defended through recourse to the example of the Prophet's companions, who reportedly walked in the shadow of these monuments themselves and yet never apparently launched any campaign for their destruction.[6]

Diverse encounters with pre-Islamic pasts in early Muslim history are also evident in artifacts, architecture, and textual traditions from many other parts of what is today identified as the "Arab World." During the Abbasid period, we find Muslim rulers figuring prominently in narratives of encounter and engagement with ruins across the region. Stories circulated of the caliph al-Maʾmun's entrance into the pyramid at Cheops, retold with considerable elaboration in the *1,001 Nights* (Cooperson 2004). Less well known, perhaps, is the visit of the caliph al-Mutawakkil to Hims. The tenth-century *Kitab al-Ghurabaʾ* (*The Book of Strangers: Medieval Arabic Graffiti on the Theme of Nostalgia* 1999, 58–59) relates that there the Commander of the Faithful "camped in a place between great churches and ancient ruins, which are pleasant to behold, and which the visitor does not want to leave."[7] The renowned fourteenth-century historian Ibn Khaldun was also fascinated by the abandoned remains of ancient structures and cities that he saw stretching from North Africa to the Arabian Peninsula. Robert Irwin (2003) has argued that such ruins in fact served as an important framework for his thinking about the civilizations that came before Islam, and what had become of them, in his massive work of historical scholarship.

Buried Treasure and More Accessible Artifacts

Some of the earliest surviving written sources for Islamic history—including the *Sira* ("Narrative" of the Prophet's biography) of Ibn Ishaq—present narratives of buried treasure found at the pre-Islamic sanctuary at Mecca (Guillaume 1955, 45–47). According to tradition, ʿAbd al-Muttalib recovered a number of remarkable ancient objects when excavating the well of Zamzam within the sacred precincts. This treasure included swords, armor, and two gazelles made of gold. In his study of this textual tradition,

Brannon Wheeler (2006, 11) has highlighted the ways in which this story draws "extensively on a number of ancient and late antique motifs, such as the burial of the temple implements, the divine origins of weapons, and the king as guardian of the sanctuary."

Fascination with the treasures of the past remained a distinct theme in the work of some of the most prominent thinkers of medieval Islam. For example, the renowned ninth-century philosopher, Ya'qub al-Kindi, wrote two works on astrological methods for finding and recovering buried treasure—in what might be seen as a rather self-serving interest in accessing the riches of the past (Burnett et al. 1997). The fifteenth-century Mamluk historian al-Maqrizi embraced such methodologies in support of his project to recover the past greatness—wealth, wisdom, and scientific knowledge—of ancient Egypt, which he believed to be buried and simply awaiting discovery beneath its sands (Irwin 2003, 227). Beyond the written page, ideas about and religious associations with buried treasure were also reflected in the construction and veneration of "long graves" of the type that can be found in sites stretching from Arabia to Southeast Asia (Wheeler 2006, 118).[8]

Treasures of the past, however, were not only believed to be buried and inaccessible—as others were visible and on display to Muslims in a number of cultural contexts. Across the Muslim world, religious sites were not only places of worship but also sometimes locations at which artifacts and elements of earlier built heritage were preserved and presented to believers in complex visual contexts. For example, in the grave complexes of Wali Songo (the "Nine Saints" traditionally associated with the Islamization of Java) are found many objects that both contribute to the aesthetic ornamentation of the venerated tombs and preserve materials indexing their pre-Islamic pasts, as well as their complex histories as Muslim religious sites as they developed over subsequent centuries. At the shrine of Sunan Bonang at Tuban (East Java) were preserved two stone *linga*s and an ornamented *yoni* (stylized representations of male and female genitalia, respectively) pedestal from an earlier Hindu sanctuary on the site,[9] as well as numerous later Islamicate artifacts, including porcelain plates decorated with Arabic script embedded into the walls and entrance gate to the cemetery.[10] Perhaps the most striking object preserved at the site, however, is a large, ornately detailed wooden sculpture depicting a forested mountain landscape dotted with buildings associated with local traditions of asceticism and pre-Islamic religious practice.[11]

Mosques have also functioned as repositories of special objects-physical points of connection and visual evocations of the complex pasts of many Muslim communities. In some striking cases, these objects originated as spoils of past wars.[12] Famous examples of this include the Quwwat al-Islam mosque in Delhi. However other, lesser known, cases can be found all across the world. One particularly striking example can be found in Malabar—a region of southern India that was at the forefront of confrontations between the Portuguese and local Muslim (and Hindu) communities in the sixteenth century (Dale 1980; Makhdoom I 2012; Makhdum 2012; Muhammad 2015). Along this stretch of the Kerala coast there stands an old wooden mosque containing a minbar, of which the back of the top step is comprised of an ornate panel said to be part of a "holy chair" taken in battle against the Portuguese. At its center is an image of the Virgin Mary, the face of which has—rather delicately—been flattened out. While thus literally "defaced" in conformity with dominant interpretations of the proscription of figural images in Islamic devotional settings, the object is, however, otherwise not disfigured (though it is discreetly covered by a curtain during prayer times).[13] Other artifacts from the same mosque include pieces of cannon shot of various sizes in both stone and iron, a shield suspended by a chain from the ceiling, and an ornamental European sword. The last of these items also serves a ritual purpose—as it is used as the staff held by the *khatib* (preacher) during the sermons accompanying Friday congregational prayers.

Swords and other weapons are used in this way in a number of historical mosques in other parts of the Muslim world as well. On the opposite coast of southern India, antique swords can be found at several older mosques in Tamil Nadu. Examples held at mosques in Kayalpatnam include that of the Rettaikullampalli (Mika'il Mosque), which was recovered along with a porcelain dish during the dredging of a tank in the yard, and another at the Khutba Sirupalli (Jami' al-Saghir) that is used as a ritual staff by the *khatib* (preacher) during Friday congregational prayers (Shokoohy 2011, 107). Across the Bay of Bengal in Indonesia, the old mosque of Kasunyatan in Banten (West Java) has an antique iron sword prop modeled after *dhu'l-fiqar* (the double-bladed sword gifted to Imam Ali by the Prophet) that is likewise used during Friday services. Elsewhere in West Java one finds iron-tipped spears used in the same way, such as the preacher's staff at the old Kejaksan mosque in Cirebon. These objects of diverse material forms and geographic origins serve in multiple ways, ranging from liturgical functions to signifiers of communal memory, and become invested with meanings that both coincide with and go beyond dominant conceptions of "heritage" in contemporary global discourses.

A new perspective on the complex cultural and historical legacies of Muslim communities that captures some of the dynamism and complexities of such engagements with pre-Islamic pasts has been developed by Shahab Ahmed in his posthumous magnum opus. His hermeneutical and "explorative" approach provides means for a new appreciation of the ways in which "Muslims *acting as Muslims*" have engaged in processes of "meaning making in terms of Islam" (Ahmed 2016, 357). Ahmed's model opens new ways to understand the significance of historical Muslim engagements with their pre-Islamic pasts that both complicates and constructively expands popular understandings of "heritage." In his discussion of the philosophical legacies of ancient Greece, for example, he argues for a conception of dynamic and accumulative tradition in which—as he provocatively poses it—"That Aristotle and Plato were not *Muslims* is simply irrelevant to their meaningful designation as *Islamic*." (Ahmed 2016, 347) Across a range of other examples from diverse fields including medicine, poetry, and the visual arts, Ahmed develops a vision of Islam as an "idiom" that allows for a more nuanced appreciation of the ways in which elements of pre-Islamic cultures have been reconstituted through the experiences of Islamization. (Ahmed 2016, 323–325)

As Islamic civilization continued to expand across Africa and Asia over the medieval and early modern periods, so did the range of ways in which Muslims came to embrace elements of their pre-Islamic pasts. This included a number of cases of appropriation wherein sites came to be reimagined in relation to "Abrahamic" tradition, such as "Adam's Peak" in present-day Sri Lanka. This site, just off the maritime trade routes from the Red Sea to Asia, was visited by Ibn Battuta in the fourteenth century as well as other Muslims in motion across the Indian Ocean since the Medieval Period (Alam and Subrahmanyam 2007, 148–149; Ibn Battuta 1994, 848–850). Along those same eastern routes, however, Muslims encountered the material cultures of diverse civilizations that had evolved wholly outside the Abrahamic framework of Islamic revelation history that was dominant across much of the Near East and the Mediterranean world. These strange new worlds engendered a wide range of responses. In his encyclopedic notes on the diverse branches of learning and literature available to Muslim readers of his day, the tenth-century Baghdadi bookseller Ibn Nadim was able to relate a number of reports in Arabic on what were at that time un-Islamized lands of India, China, and Southeast Asia—including the large and wondrous "temples of idols" found at Qimar (Angkor, in present-day Cambodia) and al-Sanf (Champa, in present-day Vietnam; Dodge 1970, 830). At about the same time, the Arab geographer Abu'l-Faraj provided his readers with a nuanced approach to how such religious images were supposedly understood and engaged in diverse ways by various non-Muslim communities (Nainar 2011, 105).

Over the centuries that followed, some of these Asian societies on the expanding frontiers of Islam eventually became Muslim themselves. In such contexts, emerging Muslim communities renegotiated their own relationships to more proximate non-Muslim pasts, where—unlike the case in Egypt—the ancient monuments of these landscapes were not signs of distant mysteries indexed to Islamic scripture, but bereft of cultural continuity with contemporary Muslim communities. Rather, they were more often tangible markers of a past that was not completely forgotten over the more recent and gradual conversion of local populations to Islam. Even in contexts of religious conquest along these new frontiers, however, Muslims were not uniformly crusading to destroy the physical embodiments of pre-Islamic culture and religious practice. As Carl Ernst (2000) has demonstrated in his study of an early seventeenth-century Persian text describing the Hindu cave temples of Ellora, an author characterized as exhibiting a "basically conservative Muslim attitude" toward religious innovation was nonetheless not only able to appreciate the aesthetic and political importance of the site, but even went so far as to chastise Sultan ʿAli ʿAdil Shah for the destruction of other Hindu temples in Vijayanagar.

Further along the routes of Islam's eastward expansion, the Indonesian island of Java was the site of a "Hindu-Buddhist" kingdom that fell to a confederation of Muslim maritime port polities on the north coast in the sixteenth century (Pigeaud 1976). Both before and since, aspects of local pre-Islamic heritage have played a major role in defining the culture of Javanese Muslims (Ricklefs 2003). This is perhaps most apparent today in aspects of nonmaterial or "intangible" cultural heritage such as music, dance, puppetry, and literature patronized as court arts by the sultans of Java to this day (Florida 1995; Headley 2004; Pigeaud 1938; Sears 1996; Sumarsam 1995). The perseverance of such traditions has sometimes been characterized in terms of "pagan survivals" by anthropologists, historians, and modern religious reformists (albeit in the service of rather different respective agendas)—who viewed them as somehow compromising the "orthodox" Islamic credentials of local Muslim communities in Java. However the appropriation, preservation, and reinterpretation of pre-Islamic traditions is by no means exceptional in the history of Islamic civilization. In fact, similar discourses can be traced in the histories of many Muslim societies across Asia, Africa, and the Middle East through the medieval and early-modern periods as well.

Narrative Traditions and Textualized Traces of the Ancients

During the early centuries of Islamic history, narrative textual traditions developed in Arabic that involved the selective appropriation and deployment of elements from Jewish, Christian, and ancient Near Eastern literatures in order to fill out and enhance the lacunae characteristic of tellings of stories involving characters and events related in the Qur'an that were shared with these earlier traditions. This body of collected narrative material has come to be referred to in Arabic as *isra'iliyyat*, and it was often used as an aid in interpreting the Qur'anic text for generations of Muslims after the death of Muhammad as a subfield of Qur'anic exegesis (*tafsir*). While some commentators have critiqued or attempted to deny the validity of these older traditions, they were accepted by many scholars and laymen for centuries as a valuable legacy to aid Muslims in their attempts to contextualize and interpret the text of Qur'anic revelation.

Such use of this earlier literary heritage has, however, come to be widely rejected by many Muslim scholars and exegetes of later historical periods. We are thus led to ask how we might understand its importance for earlier generations of Muslims who lived in contexts much more historically proximate to the Prophet himself, and to consider the reasons for this shift in dominant views on this aspect of pre-Islamic heritage. To some extent, this reflects broader trends in Islamic thought and Muslim popular culture, which have increasingly tended over the later centuries toward a more exclusively scripturalist approach to "religion," and an increasing suspicion of "tradition" (Calder 1993). These developments, in turn, may also reflect something of a modern sense of the perceived stature of "Islam" vis-à-vis other cultures in the modern world under threat. In the premodern period an expanding Islamic civilization often dealt with elements of the other cultures it encountered from a position of strength, allowing Muslims the privilege of not only "tolerating," but actively preserving, transmitting, interpreting, and even incorporating elements of those traditions within a more expansive frame. The sense of cultural confidence that enabled such engagements with pre-Islamic pasts has, however, been significantly compromised by experiences of European imperialism.

Medieval Muslim appropriations and appreciations of the heritage of earlier civilization are often discussed in terms of "science" (broadly conceived), as in the frequent references made by both academic historians and in popular apologetics about the ways in which works of philosophy, mathematics, geography, medicine, and other fields of learning from "foreign civilizations" that had been translated into Arabic during the Abbasid period were developed and transmitted. In this, some important dynamics of medieval Muslim culture could be likened to that of some European thinkers during the Renaissance. For example, in his *Genealogia Deorum Gentilium* (On the Genealogy of the Gods of the Gentiles), Boccaccio argued against what was at the time dominant Christian doctrine that rejected the literary works of antiquity, along with the "pagan" gods and goddesses they depicted. Rather, he stressed that such works remained valuable as sources through which readers could appreciate "certain natural truths…together with the deeds and moral civilization of the Ancients" (Osgood 1956, 12). Such an appreciation, he emphasized, was possible precisely because of the confidence of European Christian civilization in his day, or in his own words: " today…our strength is very great; the universally hateful doctrine of paganism has been cast into utter and perpetual darkness, and the Church in triumph holds the fortress of the enemy. Thus there is the very slightest danger in the study and investigation of paganism" (Osgood 1956, 124).

Perhaps the most well-known example of a similar openness toward the heritage of pre-Islamic literature and learning in Muslim history is that of medieval Persia, in which a new "Islamicate" form of that language was put in the service of both preserving and giving new expression to classic works, including the epic tales of the country's ancient kings. While this literary tradition has been widely discussed and highly regarded by many scholars of Persia's Muslim history, analogous traditions in other Islamicate vernaculars have not generally received such widespread attention and appreciation. Casting a wider comparative view across such material, however, can give us a more developed sense of the diverse ways in which Muslims have come to understand and live with their diverse pre-Islamic pasts.

In surviving premodern texts from the Indonesian archipelago, for example, we find vivid instances of older Indic literary sources being used in the explication of proper Islamic doctrine. In a Javanese literary text known as the *Serat Cabolek*, a debate over the purportedly "heretical" teachings of a shaykh named Haji Mutamakin concludes with the victory of his court opponents, who framed their condemnation of Mutamakin's professed rejection of the outward forms of the Shari'a through arguments supported by their own eloquent recitation of Old Javanese 'Hindu' poetry

(Ricklefs 2014; Soebardi 1975). Here, the wisdom of Java's pre-Islamic ancients was deployed to define the very norms of Islamic 'orthodoxy in a condmenation of apparent docrtinal error.'

Other Javanese texts, such as the early-nineteenth-century *Serat Centhini*, present images of Muslim travelers wandering across the island to visit religious schools, consult with rural ascetics and holy men, and visit the ruins of Hindu and Buddhist temples.[14] At such sites, the protagonists often meet with local guides and/or gurus who not only point out interesting ornamental features of pre-Islamic religious monuments but also expound upon their sources of inspiration and spiritual meanings. High on Central Java's Dieng Plateau, for example, Ki Gunawan instructs his guests (and readers of the text) about the symbolism of characters from Javanese tellings of the Sanskrit epic *Mahabharata* (Serat Centhini 2015, 431–460). In another section of the *Serat Centhini* (*i* 2015, II: 90), we find Mas Cabolang and his companions slowly making their way up and around the seven ascending levels of the great Buddhist temple mountain of Borobudur, wondering as they go at the statuary and reliefs as one of them exclaims, "If only there were someone who could explain the stories, how happy I would be!"[15] The following day, the caretaker of the nearby Candi Mendut guides the travelers to this smaller temple, which the text describes as having a roof "in the shape of a mosque," and where they are overwhelmed by the sense of the divine calm they feel in the presence of the great seated Buddha image in the inner chamber, where they decide to spend the night (*Serat Centhini— Dituturkan Ulang oleh Agus Wahyudi* 2015, II: 91).[16] These same companions later went on to visit the ruins of Hindu temples at Candi Sewu and Prambanan, where they gazed upon the relief carvings of topless women, and took in the scent of perfumed oils that continued to be poured on its statues as offerings by peddlers and prostitutes visiting these pre-Islamic sanctuaries on market days in search of good fortune. The text's protagonists then comment ambivalently on the devotion displayed to such graven images (Serat Centhini 2015, 123–135).[17]

These and other monuments to Java's pre-Islamic past have served as sites of pilgrimage throughout the island's later history, and in fact many have become even more popular destinations for both ritual and recreational purposes over recent decades. Such continuity of royal and religious sites after conversion to Islam is however not, as some have claimed, a mark of "Javanese exceptionalism."[18] Rather, analogous cultural dynamics form well-established patterns across the Muslim world. High-profile examples include "World Heritage" sites such as the Church of the Holy Wisdom, re-designated as a mosque (Aya Sofia) following the Ottoman conquest of Constantinople. But examples can be found all across the routes of Islam's expansion. These monuments, moreover, are not only about conquest and destruction—for they also open windows onto the myriad ways in which dynamic interactions with pre-Islamic cultures contributed to the development of the many rich local traditions of vernacular Muslim expression that have developed in diverse societies alongside processes of Islamization.

Academic debates and public polemics concerning the takeover of sacred spaces and the use of *spolia* from pre-Islamic temples for the building of mosques have been particularly sharp in India. With one of the largest Muslim populations in the world—despite their status as a national minority—India has been the site of complex Muslim histories of contact, exchange, settlement, and conversion. The presence of Muslims in India stretches back to the earliest periods of Islamic history, when Muslim traders began sailing across the Arabian Sea and settling in communities along the coasts (Prange 2009; Wink 1999, 67–86). The earliest surviving purpose-built Islamic religious buildings in South Asia—documented by Mehrdad Shokoohy at Bhadresvar in Gujarat—were constructed in the twelfth century by local Indian craftsmen who employed traditional construction techniques and styles of ornamentation. In these new Muslim religious buildings, they incorporated monolithic columns of alternating geometric registers, reminiscent of *linga* shafts found in Hindu temples of the region (Gravely 2006), while also integrating new elements imported to South Asia from other Muslim societies, including semicircular arches and hypostyle floor plans (Shokoohy 1988, 40). Similar dynamics informed the construction of other Indian mosques over the centuries that followed, particularly in the southern coastal regions of Malabar and Tamil Nadu (Shokoohy 2011; Tusa Fels 2011). In both cases, vernacular styles of mosque architecture developed that drew heavily upon their respective regional pre-Islamic traditions—but did so through the work of local craftsmen who created new, purpose-built mosques, rather than re-purposing materials looted from temples to pre-Islamic deities.

In some other parts of South Asia, however, Islamization followed in the path of military conquest coming down from the north, as in the case of the Ghaznavid expansion of the tenth through twelfth centuries. The historiography of Sultan Mahmud's campaigns—and his destruction of the temple at Somnath in particular—inform powerful narratives of iconoclasm that continue to shape cultural and political debates on Islam and its relation to pre-Islamic pasts today. As Jamal Elias (2012, 136) has argued in his critical examination of these discourses, however, "There is ample evidence to suggest that Muslim social elites did not see statues of Hindu gods as threatening or taboo in ways that always necessitated their destruction." He then points to other important factors involved that served to support arguments for preserving pre-Islamic religious sites and artifacts, including appreciations of their value as mirabilia and "the potential economic benefit of leaving temples and their cultures of pilgrimage intact, and in many cases Muslim rulers preferred to keep the idols as a source of revenue" (Elias 2012, 132). More recently, Waleed Ziad (2016) has provided striking new evidence in support of this last point in particular through his studies of a cache of Arabic-inscribed copper coins from a Hindu temple in Gandhara.

All through the history of Islamic expansion in South Asia, moreover, Muslims interacted with local cultures to together produce a remarkable range of new artistic, architectural, and literary monuments, which incorporated contributions by Muslims and non-Muslims alike. Today the heritage of creative fusion that produced these Indian Muslim vernacular traditions faces sharp criticism from several different religious groups espousing agendas of both theological and aesthetic "purification." Over recent decades some vocal segments of the Hindu Right in India have developed a popular discourse of rejection of what they deem to be the "pollution" brought to Mother India by the "foreign" invasions of "Persian" and "Turkish" Muslims. At the same time, a growing number of Muslims have become increasingly uncomfortable with aspects of their own heritage that appear to draw from the pre-Islamic cultural traditions of their communities, resulting in the disappearance of vernacular traditions of architecture and ornament, and their replacement by forms imagined to project more "universal"—as opposed to "vernacular"—standards of an Islamic aesthetic.

Across southern India today, for example, we witness the rapid eclipse of traditional styles of vernacular mosque architecture as an increasing number of such buildings that have been identified by both international scholars and local cultural NGO activists as major monuments to the region's Muslim vernacular built heritage are being torn down by some members of their own religious communities and replaced by new structures of concrete and re-bar. Most often these new mosques are being built in rather plain styles, although usually with the addition of a minaret and/or a dome to prominently mark its exterior form as "Islamic." Speaking with people in some of these communities, the reasons given for such destruction and radically different reconstructions are often "practical" ones—including the need for more prayer space and/or the material decay of earlier wooden or cut-stone structures. Transformations of the architectural profiles of communities in southern India, however, also reflect broader shifts in Islamic religious sensibilities influenced by currents of modernizing reform, which have gained ground across many parts of the Muslim world since the latter decades of the twentieth century. These modern intellectual and ideological developments have had significant effects on conceptions of identity in relation to the material culture and built heritage of a number of Muslim communities.

In the early decades of the twentieth century a number of prominent Egyptians had positively pointed toward the ruins of their country's pre-Islamic past in defining modern visions of nationalism (Wood 1998). However, reference to the monuments of the Pharaonic past (and the evocation of ancient styles in modern structures) as symbols of national pride have since become distinctly problematic for many of its modern citizens. Whereas some early Egyptian nationalists appealed to the monuments of the Pharaonic age as markers of a proud regional distinction, the assassin of Anwar Sadat in 1981 proclaimed to have "killed Pharaoh!" Such dramatic redeployments of the symbolism of the cultural heritage of pre-Islamic pasts track alongside the rise of political Islamist movements, Salafi scripturalism, and *da'wa* (proselytizing of Islam) projects of religious revival across much of the Muslim world since the 1970s.

Rejection of pre-Islamic heritage as symbols for contemporary Muslim communities are often expressed in the language of "purification" prominent in many major streams of modern religious reformism, from the Salafi scripturalism popularized by Rashid Rida, to Sayyid Qutb's clarion call for the rejection of *jahiliyya* (barbarism) in all its forms, and the post–petrol boom Saudi sponsorship of scripturalist reform projects around the world. The calls of such modern reform movements to distance contemporary Muslims from both what they see as "innovations" or "accretions" of the histories of their communities, as well as survivals from the "pagan" heritage of their pre-Islamic pasts, have themselves been evolving over the past century, following the Geist of a changing political climate. Since the second half of the twentieth century, Muslim discourses have taken shape around what are believed by some to be more exclusively "Islamic" conceptions of legitimate heritage—from modern Arabic conceptions of *turath* ("heritage") to Malaysian discourse on *tamaddun Islami* ("Islamic Civilization"). These discourses have tended to marginalize, and in many cases to actively denigrate, elements of heritage grounded in the pre-Islamic pasts of Muslim communities—while introducing new and increasingly influential models of Muslim antagonism toward pre-Islamic pasts that stand in sharp contrast to that presented in the discussion above of Shahab Ahmed's (2016) reading of earlier historical experiences of meaning making.

Over recent decades such shifts in meanings ascribed to pre-Islamic cultural legacies can be tracked across many parts of the broader Muslim world, and not only toward surviving stone statues and monuments. In Indonesia, for example, popular modes of cultural practice associated with local traditions came to be pejoratively labeled as *abangan* ("Javanist," or only "nominally Muslim"), and those so labeled came under increasing pressure to "purify" their understanding of religion by rejecting association with perceived "survivals" of their pre-Islamic cultural heritage (Ricklefs 2012, 371–407). Recent violent Muslim reactions against the symbols of pre-Islamic pasts include the calls of Indonesian Islamists for the dismantling of Borobudur,[19] the smashing of Buddha images at the Museum of the Maldives in 2012,[20] the much-publicized demolition of the monumental Buddha images at Bamiyan by the Taliban in 2001,[21] as well as the recent and ongoing destruction of both medieval Muslim and earlier pre-Islamic monuments in areas of the Middle East under the control of the Islamic State. This rising wave of destruction has fostered a growing sense of threat among those concerned with heritage over the fate of sites in the Muslim world. It is in this context that the International Criminal Court in The Hague has recently made its first ever conviction for the destruction of historical buildings as a war crime.[22]

At the same time, however, there is also a need to recognize evidence of a more positive appreciation of pre-Islamic pasts among contemporary Muslims in several countries. Even Saudi Arabia—a country's whose official interpretation of Islam places great emphasis on purification—has, for example, supported ground-breaking archaeological work at pre-Islamic sites including Qaryat al-Faw. This work has resulted in the discovery and publication of striking artifacts reflecting the reception and vernacularization of Hellenistic culture in the Arabian Peninsula during the early centuries of the Common Era, which has served to significantly reshape our picture of the religious and cultural contexts of Arabia before the rise of Islam.[23] Arab engagements with the pre-Islamic culture of Mediterranean Hellenism clearly continued well after the rise of Islam, as evidenced by the late eighth-century mosaics of Umm al-Resas and the paintings of the Qusayr ʿAmra in Jordan. Monuments such as these reflect in striking ways how some of the earliest generations of Muslims engaged actively and appreciatively with elements of the pre-Islamic past.[24] There are thus both well-developed precedents for—and significant new work being done today by—Muslims exploring diverse aspects of relations to their pre-Islamic heritage. The range of ways in which this has happened and continues to occur across many areas of the Muslim world demonstrate that there is no single "Islamic" approach to the concept of heritage. Rather debates about the meaning of the past for life in the present and visions of the future are dynamic discourses incorporating an expansive body of ideas and experiences across diverse communities within the Muslim world.

Notes

1. Unless otherwise noted, all translations of Qurʾanic passages in this paper are those of M.A.S. Abdel Haleem (2010).
2. *Al ʿImran* (3):137, *al-Anʿam* (6):11, *Yusuf* (12):109, *al-Nahl* (16):36, *al-Hajj* (22): 46, *al-Naml* (27):69, *al-Rum* (30):9 & 42, *al-Malaʾika* (35):44, *al-Muʾmin* (40):21 & 82, and *Muhammad* (47):10. One of these verses, *al-ʿAnkabut* (29):20, however, focuses more on nature as God's creation rather than on the ruins of human civilizations.
3. In this chapter of the Qurʾan, we also find one of the uses of the trope of "travelling through the land" in verse 109: "...Have the [disbelievers] not travelled through the land and seen the end of those who went before them?..."
4. Fodor (1970) reconstructs and presents a series of complex genealogies and narratives that relate traditions that center on Hermes, Surid, and Shaddad b. ʿAd.
5. Michael Cook (1983) has demonstrated that this tradition associating the pyramids with Hermitic wisdom tradition is not, however, continuous with local Coptic heritage, but rather something that seems to have originated elsewhere in the medieval Muslim world—particularly in Iraq—and was later introduced into conversations on Egypt's wonders among Muslims across the Middle East.
6. Indeed, it was even said that one of them had scribbled graffiti on one of the pyramid blocks. Haarmann (1980) suggests that this might still survive to this day in a bit of illegible Kufic at Abu Sir.

7. Tropes of the pleasures of visits to Christian monasteries can be traced back to the pre-Islamic period and continue through the poetry of the sixth-century Imru' al-Qays to al-Isfahani in the tenth—becoming a staple of new genres that flourished under the patronage of Muslim rulers. See, Elizabeth Key Fowden, "The Lamp and the Wine Flask, Early Muslim Interest in Christian Monasticism."
8. Perhaps the most famous of these was that associated with Eve in Jeddah—at least until its destruction in 1928. Long graves (*kubur panjang*) can be found in many parts of Southeast Asia, often at sites associated with the early history of Islamization in the region, although in many cases they may be later embellishments to earlier monuments on site. Notable examples include the royal burial complex at Pasai (Aceh, Sumatra) and in the cemetery of Fatima bint Maimun in Gresik (East Java).
9. Two simple *lingas* are still embedded in situ on either side of the gateway into the middle yard of the cemetery. The *yoni*, which had long been situated inside a large ablution pool on site, has been moved to the nearby museum on the central square of Tuban.
10. Such Arabic-script plates are found at a number of historic Muslim mosques and shrines across the region. They are, for the most part however, not ancient artifacts but generally date from the nineteenth century. Many of the most commonly found plates of this type were produced in England during the nineteenth and early twentieth centuries for an export market that included Mecca—whence they were purchased by pilgrims as souvenirs (Mols 2013). In Southeast Asia, many examples of such plates were subsequently installed as ornaments at earlier sites, including the graves of some of Java's pioneering Islamic *wali* (Chambert-Loir 2011). Other examples can be found at the Kudikhao Mosque in Bangkok—a signature monument of Thai Muslim vernacular architecture.
11. This remarkable object is now housed near the cemetery in the Museum Kembang Putih. See Rony Firman Firdaus, *Kalpataru: Media Merajut Harmoni antar Umat Beragama—Lomba Deskripsi Koleksi Unggulan se Jawa Timur Tahun (2012)*; Hélène Njoto, "À Propos d'une Pièce en Bois Sculptée de l'Art du Pasisir."
12. It should be noted, however, that in many cases observers had mislabeled as temple spolia elements that had actually been purpose-built for mosques, but executed in pre-Islamic vernacular styles. Finbarr Flood (2009, 47) remarks on this in connection with the monuments of Bhadreshvar in Gujarat. For more on the aesthetics and politics of the use of actual spolia in Islamic India, (Ibid., 121–226).
13. This striking image is generally covered with a cloth curtain, especially during prayer times.

14. The complete Javanese text has been edited and published in the original Javanese by Yayasan Centhini in Yogyakarta. Dutch and Bahasa Indonesia summaries of its contents have been published by Theodore Pigeaud, "De *Serat Tjabolang* en de *Serat Tjenthini:* Inhoudsopgaven," and Ki Sumidi Adisasmita, *Pustaka Centini: Ikhtisar Seluruh Isinya*. An Indonesian-language translation was undertaken and published in two stages, the first volumes appearing from the Balai Pustaka press (volumes 1–4), and the remainder published by Gadjah Mada University Press. It has also recently been published in an Indonesian-language adaptation: *Serat Centhini— Dituturkan Ulang oleh Agus Wahyudi*. A heavily illustrated, but textually rather loose, English overview of the text can be found in Soewito Santoso, *The Centhini Story: The Javanese Journey of Life*.
15. *Serat Centhini* - Balai Pustaka edition II: 56.
16. Serat Centhini - Balai Pustaka edition II: 57.
17. *Serat Centhini* (Cakrawala edition) III: 131–132; Balai Pustaka edition III: 87–88.
18. The adaptation of older Hindu religious sites in Southeast Asia for use by latter-day communities converted to other religions is also seen, for example, in the contemporary practice of Theravada Buddhists at the caves and rock shelters of Phnom Kulen, Cambodia. See, Helen Ibbitson Jessup, "The Rock Shelter of Peung Kumnu and Visnu Images on Phnom Kulen."
19. Islamists had carried out a bombing at Borobudur in 1985 that caused some damage. Since then there have been some sporadic calls for further destruction, but threats have significantly increased since 2014, when the Islamic State targeted this ninth-century Buddhist monument in a Facebook post. Aaron Akinyemi, "Isis Threat to Ancient Buddhist Temple Puts Indonesia Police on Alert."
20. This was not the first act of modern Maldivian Muslim iconoclasm. A large Buddha statue discovered on a 1959 expedition to the island of Thoddu was first decapitated by a member of the local community before being brought back to the presidential palace at Malé, where vandals smashed it completely to bits within a week. See, Robinson, *The Maldives: Islamic Republic, Tropical Autocracy*, 131.
21. On this act of destruction in relation to both deeper historical dynamics of Muslim iconoclasm and contemporary political contexts, see Elias, "Un/Making Idolatry: From Meccas to Bamiyan."
22. On September 27, 2016, Ahmad al-Faqi al-Mahdi was convicted over the 2012 destruction of a mosque and nine mausoleums in Timbuktu (Male). See, Camila Domonoske, "For First Time, Destruction of Cultural Sites Leads to War Crime Conviction."

23. For an overview of recent archaeological work on the pre-Islamic Arabian Peninsula, see: *Roads of Arabia: Archaeology and History of the Kingdom of Saudi Arabia*.
24. On this site, see Garth Fowden, *Qusayr 'Amra: Art and the Ummayad Elite in Late Antique Syria*.

Bibliography

Abdel Haleem, M.A.S. 2010. *The Qur'an: English Translation, with Parallel Arabic Text*. Oxford: Oxford University Press.
Adisasmita, Ki Sumidi. 1975. *Pustaka Centini: Ikhtisar Seluruh Isinya*. Yogyakarta: U.P. Indonesia.
Ahmed, Shahab. 2016. *What Is Islam? The Importance of Being Islamic*. Princeton, NJ: Princeton University Press.
Akinyemi, Aaron. 2014. "Isis Threat to Ancient Buddhist Temple Puts Indonesia Police on Alert." 23 August. http://www.ibtimes.co.uk/isis-threat-ancient-buddhist-temple-puts-indonesia-police-alert-1462352
Alam, Muzaffar, and Sanjay Subrahmanyam 2007. *Indo-Persian Travels in the Age of Discoveries*. Cambridge: Cambridge University Press.
Ali, Abdullah Yusuf. 1938. *The Holy Qur-an: Text, Translation, and Commentary*. 3rd ed. Kashmiri Bazar, Lahore: Shaik Muhammad Ashraf.
Burnett, Charles, Keiji Yamamoto, and Michio Yano 1997. "Al-Kindi on Finding Buried Treasure." *Arabic Sciences and Philosophy* no. 7: 57–90.
Calder, Norman. 1993. "Tafsir from Tabari to Ibn Kathir: Problems in the Description of a Genre, Illustrated with Reference to the Story of Abraham." In *Approaches to the Qur'an*, edited by Gerald R. Hawting and Abdel-Kader A. Shareef, 101–140. London: Routledge.
Chambert-Loir, Henri. 2011. "Melahap Teks: Piring-Piring Inggris Berhiasan Sajak Melayu." In *Sultan, Pahlawan dan Hakim*, edited by Henri Chambert-Loir. Jakarta, Indonesia: Kepustakaan Populer Gramedia.
Cook, Michael. 1983. "Pharaonic History in Medieval Egypt." *Studia Islamica* no. 57: 67–103.
Cooperson, Michael. 2004. "Al-Ma'mun, the Pyramids, and the Hieroglyphs." In *Abbasid Studies II: Occasional Papers of the School of 'Abbasid Studies, Leuven, 20 June–1 July, 2004*, edited by John Nawas, 165–190. Leuven, Belgium: Peeters.
Crone, Patricia and Shmuel Moreh. 1999. *The Book of Strangers: Medieval Arabic Graffiti on the Theme of Nostalgia*. Princeton, NJ: Markus Wiener.
Dale, Stephen Frederic. 1980. *Islamic Society on the South Asian Frontier: The Mappilas of Malabar, 1498–1922*. Oxford: Clarendon Press.

Dodge, Bayard. 1970. *The Fihrist of al-Nadim*. Vol. 2. New York: Columbia University Press.
Domonoske, Camila. 2016. "For First Time, Destruction of Cultural Sites Leads to War Crime Conviction." *Nationa Public Radio*, 27 September. http://www.npr.org/sections/thetwo-way/2016/09/27/495606932/for-first-time-destruction-of-cultural-sites-leads-to-war-crime-conviction?sc=17&f=&utm_source=iosnewsapp&utm_medium=Email&utm_campaign=app.
Elias, Jamal J. 2007. "(Un)making Idolatry: From Mecca to Bamiyan." *Future Anterior: Journal of Historic Preservation, History, Theory, and Criticism* no. 4 (2): 12–29.
Elias, Jamal J. 2012. *Aisha's Cushion: Religious Art, Perception, and Practice in Islam*. Cambridge, MA: Harvard University Press.
Ernst, Carl W. 2000. "Admiring the Works of the Ancients: The Ellora Temple as Viewed by Indo-Muslim Authors." In *Beyond Turk and Hindu: Rethinking Religious Identities in Islamicate South Asia*, edited by David Gilmartin and Bruce B. Lawrence, 98–120. Gainesville: University Press of Florida.
Firman Firdaus, Rony 2012. *Kalpataru: Media Merajut Harmoni antar Umat Beragama—Lomba Deskripsi Koleksi Unggulan se Jawa Tumur Tahun 2012*. Tuban, Indonesia: UPTD Museum Kembang Putih.
Flood, Finbarr B. 2009. *Objects of Translation: Material Culture and Medieval "Hindu-Muslim" Encounter*. Princeton, NJ: Princeton University Press.
Florida, Nancy. 1995. *Writing the Past, Inscribing the Future: History as Prophecy in Colonial Java*. Durham, NC: Duke University Press.
Fodor, Alexander. 1970. "The Origins of the Arabic Legends of the Pyramids." *Acta Orientalia Academiae Hungaricae* no. 23 (3): 335–363.
Fowden, Elizabeth Key. 2007. "The Lamp and the Wine Flask, Early Muslim Interest in Christian Monasticism." In *Islamic Crosspollinations: Interactions in the Medieval Middle East*, edited by Anna Akasoy, James E. Montgomery, and Peter E. Pormann, 1–28. Exeter, UK: Gibb Memorial Trust.
Fowden, Garth. 2004. *Qusayr 'Amra: Art and the Umayyad Elite in Late Antique Syria*. Berkeley: University of California Press.
Frank, Ute and Joachim Gierlichs, in collaboration with Sophia Vasilopoulou and Lucia Wagner. 2010. *Roads of Arabia: Archaeology and History of the Kingdom of Saudi Arabia*. Paris: Somogyi Art Publishers.
Ghabban, Ali Ibrahim, Béatrice André-Salvini, Françoise Demange, Carine Juvin, and Marianne Cotty 2010. *Roads of Arabia: Archaeology and History of the Kingdom of Saudi Arabia*. Paris: Somogyi Art Publishers.
Gravely, Frederick H. 2006. *An Outline of Indian Temple Architecture*. Chennai, India: Government Museum.
Guillaume, Alfred. 1955. *The Life of Muhammad: A Translation of Ibn Ishaq's Sirat Rasul Allah*. Oxford: Oxford University Press.

Haarmann, Ulrich. 1978. "Die Sphinx: Synkretistische Volksreligiosität im Spätmittelalterlichen Islamischen Ägypten." *Saeculum: Jahrbuch für Universalgeschichte* no. 29: 367-384.
Haarmann, Ulrich. 1980. "Regional Sentiment in Medieval Egypt." *Bulletin of the School of Oriental and African Studies* no. 43 (1): 55-66.
Haarmann, Ulrich. 1991a. "In Quest of the Spectacular: Noble and Learned Visitors to the Pyramids around 1200 A.D." In *Islamic Studies Presented to Charles J. Adams*, edited by Wael Hallaq and Donald P. Little, 57-67. Leiden, Netherlands: Brill.
Haarmann, Ulrich. 1991b. "Misalla." In *The Encyclopedia of Islam*, Second edition, 140-141. Leiden, Netherlands: Brill.
Haarmann, Ulrich. 1996. "Medieval Muslim Perceptions of Pharaonic Egypt." In *Ancient Egyptian Literature: History and Forms*, edited by Antonio Loprieno. Leiden, Netherlands: Brill.
Headley, Stephen. 2004. *Durga's Mosque: Cosmology, Conversion, and Community in Central Javanese Islam*. Singapore: ISEAS Press.
Ibn Battuta. 1994. *The Travels of Ibn Battuta, A.D. 1325-1354 - Translated by H.A.R. Gibb with revisions and notes from the Arabic text edited by C. Defrémery and B.R. Sanguinetti*. Vol. London: The Hakluyt Society.
Irwin, Robert. 2003. "Al-Maqrizi and Ibn Khuldun: Historians of the Unseen." *Mamluk Studies Review* no. 7 (2): 217-230.
Jessup, Helen Ibbitson. 2008. "The Rock Shelter of Peung Kumnu and Visnu Images on Phnom Kulen." In *Interpreting Southeast Asia's Past: Monument, Image, Text*, edited by Elisabeth A. Bacus, Ian C. Glover, and Peter D. Sharrock. Singapore: National University of Singapore Press.
Makhdoom I, Zainuddin 2012. *Tahrid Ahlil Imam ala Jihadi Abdati Sulban*. Calicut, India: Other Books.
Makhdum, Zainuddin. 2012. *Tuhfat al-Mujahidin: A Historical Epic of the Sixteenth Century*. Calicut, India: Other Books.
Mols, Luitgard. 2013. *Verlangen naar Mekka: De Hadj in Honderd Voorwerpen*. Leiden, Netherlands: Rijksmuseum Volkenkunde.
Muhammad, Qadi. 2015. *Fath al-Mubin: A Contemporary Account of the Portuguese Invasion of Malabar in Arabic Verse*. Calicut, India: Other Books.
Nainar, Muhammad Husayn. 2011. *Arab Geographers' Knowledge of Southern India*. Calicut, India: Other Books.
Njoto, Hélène. 2014. "À Propos d'une Pièce en Bois Sculptée de l'Art du Pasisir (XVeS.-XVIIeS.): Le 'Kalpataru' du Musée de Tuban à Java-Est." *Archipel* no. 88: 169-188.
Osgood, Charles G. 1956. *Boccaccio on Poetry*. New York: Library of Liberal Arts.
Pigeaud, Theodore G. 1933. "De Serat Tjabolang en de Serat Tjenthini. Inhoudsopgaven." *Verhandelingen van het Bataviaasch Genootschap* no. 72 (2): 1-89.

Pigeaud, Theodore G. 1938. *Javaanse Volksvertoningen: Bijdrage tot de Beschrijving van Land en Volk*. Batavia (Jakarta, Indonesia): Volkslectuur.

Pigeaud, Theodore G. 1976. *Islamic States in Java 1500–1700: A Summary of Eight Dutch Books and Articles by Dr. H.J. de Graaf*. The Hague, Netherlands: Martinus Nijhoff.

Prange, Sebastian R. 2009. "Like Banners on the Sea: Muslim Trade Networks and Islamization in Malabar and Maritime Southeast Asia." In *Islamic Connections: Muslim Societies in South and Southeast Asia*, edited by R. Michael Feener and Terenjit Sevea, 25–47. Singapore: ISEAS Press.

Ricklefs, Merle Calvin. 2003. *Mystic Synthesis in Java: A History of Islamicization from the Fourteenth to the Early Nineteenth Centuries*. Norwalk, CT: East Bridge.

Ricklefs, Merle Calvin. 2012. *Islamisation and Its Opponents in Java, c. 1930 to the Present*. Singapore: NUS Press.

Ricklefs, Merle Calvin. 2014. "Cabolek." In *Encyclopedia of Islam, THREE*, edited by Kate Fleet, Gudrun Krämer, Denis Matringe, John Nawas, and Everett Rowson. Leiden, The Netherlands: Brill Online.

Robinson, John J. 2015. *The Maldives: Islamic Republic, Tropical Autocracy*. London: Hurst & Company.

Santoso, Soewito. 2006. *The Centhini Story: The Javanese Journey of Life*. Singapore: Marshall Cavendish.

Sears, Laura. 1996. *Shadows of Empire: Colonial Discourses and Javanese Tales*. Durham, NC: Duke University Press.

Serat Centhini. 2015. 12 vols. Vol. 1. Yogyakarta, Indonesia: Cakrawala.

Shokoohy, Mehrdad. 2011. *Muslim Architecture of Southern India: The Sultanate of Ma`bar and the Traditions of the Maritime Settlers on the Malabar and Coromandel Coasts (Tamil Nadu, Kerala, and Goa)*. London: Routledge Curzon.

Shokoohy, Mehrdad with Contributions by Manijeh Bayani-Wolpert and Natalie H. Shokoony. 1988. *Bhadreśvar: The Oldest Islamic Monuments in India*. Leiden, Netherlands: Brill.

Soebardi, S. 1975. *The Book of Cabolek: A Critical Edition with Introduction, Translation, and Notes*. The Hague, Netherlands: Martinus Nijhoff.

Sumarsam. 1995. *Gamelan: Cultural Interaction and Musical Development in Central Java*. Chicago: University of Chicago Press.

Tusa Fels, Patricia 2011. *Mosques of Cochin*. Kochi, India: Mappin Publishing.

Wheeler, Brannon. 2006. *Mecca and Eden: Ritual, Relics, and the Territory in Islam*. Chicago: University of Chicago Press.

Wink, André. 1999. *Al-Hind: The Making of the Indo-Islamic World*. Vol. 1— Early Medieval India and the Expansion of Islam, Seventh—Eleventh centuries. New Delhi, India: Oxford University Press.

Wood, Michael. 1998. "The Use of the Pharaonic Past in Modern Egyptian Nationalism." *Journal of the American Research Center in Egypt* no. 35: 179–196.
Ziad, Waleed. 2016. "'Islamic Coins' from a Hindu Temple: Reconsidering Ghaznavid Interactions with Hindu Sacred Sites through New Numismatic Evidence from Gandhara." *Journal of the Economic and Social History of the Orient* no. 59: 618–659.

R. Michael Feener is the Sultan of Oman Fellow at the Oxford Centre for Islamic Studies, and Islamic Centre Lecturer in the History Faculty at the University of Oxford, United Kingdom. He has published extensively in the fields of Islamic studies and Southeast Asian history, as well as on post-disaster reconstruction, religion, and development. His most recent monograph is *Sharia and Social Engineering* (Oxford University Press, 2014).

Open Access This book is licensed under the terms of the Creative Commons Attribution 4.0 International License (http://creativecommons.org/licenses/by/4.0/), which permits use, sharing, adaptation, distribution and reproduction in any medium or format, as long as you give appropriate credit to the original author(s) and the source, provide a link to the Creative Commons license and indicate if changes were made.

The images or other third party material in this chapter are included in the chapter's Creative Commons license, unless indicated otherwise in a credit line to the material. If material is not included in the chapter's Creative Commons license and your intended use is not permitted by statutory regulation or exceeds the permitted use, you will need to obtain permission directly from the copyright holder.

CHAPTER 4

Reclaiming Heritage Through the Image of Traditional Habitat

Ali Mozaffari and Nigel Westbrook

Abstract From the 1960s, Iran, like many other similar countries experienced a radical urban expansion and industrialization, chiefly as a result of the expanding oil industry. Internal migration fueled by industrialization created both a crisis of habitation and a cultural dissonance, in response to which various schemes were developed for model communities, intended to bridge the gap between Iranian culture, its heritage, and modern urbanism. We will examine one such "model community," New Shushtar, a housing complex adjacent to the ancient heritage town of Shushtar, in which architectural motifs and images were used to evoke and perhaps invoke authentic traditional life. We will place this complex within the broader context in the Muslim world of attempts to defend regional culture from the effects of globalization.

Keywords Traditionalism · housing · development · Iran · Shushtar New Town

---

A. Mozaffari (✉)
Deakin University, Geelong, VIC, Australia
Curtin University, Perth, WA, Australia

N. Westbrook
University of Western Australia, Perth, WA, Australia

Introduction: The Mirage of "Islamic Housing"

In April 1978, the Aga Khan Foundation held its first symposium addressing the question of Islamic architecture and heritage, entitled "Towards an Architecture in the Spirit of Islam." In retrospect, the symposium's theme, which posited the belief in an essential Islamic identity pertaining to the material culture of Muslim societies, could be seen as a significant moment in the construction of an Islamist ideology with reference to architectural heritage. In his opening remarks, the Aga Khan, Prince Shah Karim Hussayni, noted the lack of a common position on what an appropriate architectural idiom for Islamic societies might look like, but also the dynamic social situation that these societies faced in the context of new oil wealth, decolonization, and uneven development. Nonetheless, he argued, there was a necessity for a common Islamic identity and culture (Holod 1980, viii):

> Many of these countries have emerged from a colonial era and are searching for an identity of their own. This identity is at the same time specific and regional, yet it must continue to share a common civilization and history with other Islamic countries.

Thus was succinctly stated an inherent contradiction, between a (theologically based) conception of the *umma* (the unity of world Muslims) and an acknowledgment of cultural differentiation in Islamic societies. In his presentation following these opening remarks—and echoing what would become one of the major idioms of political Islam—Seyyed Hossein Nasr, the influential traditionalist Islamic philosopher, attributed the corruption of Islamic societies to their exposure to Western secular culture and intellectual traditions; this recalled the accusation of *Gharbzadegi* (Westoxification) of earlier Iranian critical writers toward the cultural change their country was undergoing under the twentieth-century Pahlavi dynasty (Hanson 1983, 2–4). Addressing the theme of the symposium, Nasr's presentation contrasted the ugliness derived from slavish imitation of foreign models with the "serenity and beauty of the traditional Islamic city" (Holod 1980, 1). There should be a return to Islamic traditions in both cultural practices and heritage, an "emergence from darkness into the light" (Holod 1980, 5).

A common theme at this symposium was that architecture constituted a major element of the cultural heritage of Islamic cities. The challenge posed here was to develop principles that might enable new buildings to belong to and constitute that cultural heritage. Janet Abu-Lughod (Holod

1980, 61–75), for example, argued that the traditional buildings and spaces that constitute the heritage of an Islamic city should serve as models, or an underlying structure, for new developments that respond to the modern culture and economy. Thus, these new habitats might become compatible with traditional heritage, while themselves becoming constitutive of it. Abu-Lughod asserted that preserving Islamic heritage necessitated not only the preservation of significant and typical structures but also the conservation of spatial typologies (e.g., streets, small squares, courtyard housing). Architectural, and thus cultural, identity should be safeguarded by conserving past heritage while adapting habitat for present and future needs; another delegate noted that construction techniques and typologies should be appropriately adapted rather than slavishly follow past models (Holod 1980, 41). In a later article, Abu-Lughod (1987, 172–173) traced the roots of essentialist notions of the Islamic city to French orientalist sources and restricted the intrinsically Islamic characteristics of traditional Muslim cities to three factors: 1. distinction between members of the *umma* and outsiders; 2. a spatially expressed gender segregation, and 3. a devolved legal system with respect to land claims between residents (Abu Lughod 1987, 162–163). These factors, she argued, did not necessarily have a tangible, material aspect.

In the Third Aga Khan Symposium held in Jakarta in 1979, which was dedicated to the question of housing, Prince Hussayni reiterated his call to remedy a situation in which then-contemporary buildings in Islamic cities failed to "reflect or respond to Islamic tradition, thought or ways of life" (Safran 1980, xi). This type of architecture was to his mind worse than destruction of the past—the two conditions of physical and memorial obliteration resulted in a precarity that had brought the "Islamic World" toward the "brink" of identity loss (Safran 1980, xi) or a loss of cultural memory (Assmann 2011a, 2011b). On the other hand, in the face of rapid change and population growth brought about by processes of modernity, the Prince thought that Islamic forms of housing that accorded with Islamic tradition and custom were, at the time, "unattainable" (Safran 1980, x).

The discontent expressed through such statements reflects both nostalgia for a lost sense of community and concern about a destabilized sense of Muslim cultural identity. This quest for an authentic Islamic habitat, one that reflects and incorporates Islamic heritage, can be detected in both globalizing projects such as the World Heritage Organization (WHO), and in materially embedded processes, such as the local naturalization of syncretically assembled, exotic sources; it involves competing and confusing interpretations of tradition (Harrison 2015, 297–312). Thus, does an "Islamic habitat" refer to the embodiment of a continuous tradition? Is it a fictitious fabrication, an act of remembering, or a site of cultural heritage? Certainly, one of the speakers at the Aga Khan Jakarta Symposium, the Iranian architect, Kamran Diba, implied that such a habitat required a continuity with a revered past. Describing his design for housing at Shushtar No'w (Shushtar New Town) in Iran, he asserted its maintenance of a "traditional continuity," and a "tightly knit fabric reminiscent of Islamic vernacular architecture" (Safran 1980, 41–45).

Such an essentialist statement fabricates a unitary and immutable cultural identity in which present-day cultural productions derive their value through continuity with the surviving heritage of the past. In the following discussion, we will interrogate and historicize such attempts to "reclaim heritage," by building on recent concepts of remembering, tradition, heritage, and their instabilities, to then trace the genealogy of the idea of Muslim habitat. We will argue that this concept is a product of a global tendency that developed out of Western colonial and postcolonial policies and critiques, through which European modernist, technologically advanced theories of urban and regional planning were adapted and broadened to accommodate the new perspectives of sociology and anthropology in response to what was perceived to be a gradient of cultural evolution. We will further problematize the very notion of Islamic heritage in architecture, arguing that such works as Shushtar No'w may be considered as heritage, not because of some essentially Islamic character, but rather for their capacity to engender the construction of belonging—a sense of place—through evocation of traditions, images, and familiar spatial experiences, where "the past is used to legitimate a new practice, not an existing one" (Otto and Pedersen 2005, 29).

Probing an Islamic Tradition in Architecture and Habitat

The discourse of a purported Islamic heritage, as expressed through architecture and, more specifically, the idea of Islamic housing and habitat, may be explained in part through a process of memory restitution. Here, the medium of design plays an important role in coalescing, routinizing, socializing, and potentially globalizing practices, symbols, and beliefs incorporated in the "myth" of Muslim housing. Therefore, an examination of the establishment and transmission of an Islamic tradition in architecture is a process that must pay attention to both content, that which is handed down (Otto and Pedersen 2005, 22), and form, the manner of handing down. It is argued here that transmission of an Islamic heritage lies in transactions between two categories—Muslim memories and Muslim heritages—which help to frame how an Islamic habitat discourse and its heritage might be formed in dialogue with cultural memory.

The dramatic shifts and disruptions of social structures in most Muslim societies since the late nineteenth century, and most critically in the 1960s and 1970s, following successive Arab-Israeli wars, problematize this process. The undermining of political secularism and a rise of Islamic nationalism formed the context for the idea of the need for an authentic Islamic tradition and heritage in architecture and urbanism (Dorraj 1999, 237; Juergensmeyer 1993, 12). The attempt to revive and institutionalize such traditions by powerful individuals like the Aga Khan, and groups or even states, such as Iran after 1979, was based on their assumption or hope that their Muslim audiences would be willing to subscribe to the new memories and customs, or could be coerced into the routines, in part secured through the global rise of political Islam.

At the heart of this turn to tradition is the desire to construct a modern Muslim identity.[1] Once taken up by Islamist discourses in a Muslim society, a habitat ascribed as Muslim can in itself become a "site of memory" (Nora 1989, 7–24). That is to say, it can be an indication of an ethnoreligious, nationalist tendency as well as operating on a more functional—meaning lived and experienced—level of memory. In the traditional village, a semblance of timelessness was maintained by a slowly evolving symbiosis between place, economy, and culture; however, as it was drawn into a globalized economy and new sources of work were created in urban centers, this rhythm was disrupted by the internal migration of rural populations to the city fringes. It is in response to this historical and economic context that governmental policies were developed in both European colonies and emergent Middle Eastern nations, for the creation of a new habitat appropriate for these populations, one that could bridge the traditional and modern worlds.

Housing the "Indigenous" in French North Africa

Arguably, the discourse of "Islamic housing" may be traced back to the ameliorative colonial policy concerning so-called indigenous housing and settlements developed in the French protectorate of Morocco from 1912 to 1925 under Resident-General Marshal Lyautey. Lyautey sought to protect the fabric and spatial structure of traditional settlements such as the casbah of Casablanca, which were beginning to be perceived to possess heritage value given their embodiment of cultural traditions (Rabinow 1989, 277–319). These settlements were seen to have developed out of such traditional social practices as the clan structure, seclusion of women, the *waqf* (religious endowment) system, and adaptation to local climatic conditions. On the other hand, the similarity of building forms and spaces in the Jewish and Muslim quarters did, however, call into question an intrinsically Islamic habitat. Lyautey's preservationist policies did little to solve the problems of internal migration, and the formerly organic and cohesive urban structure of the old urban cores became subject to massive overcrowding, often by new residents with few cultural links to the traditional inhabitants, the merchant elite, and poorer artisans. The formerly unitary spatial and social structure was thus disrupted (Cohen and Eleb 1998, 214–226).

In subsequent years prior to the Second World War, public and company housing estates for Muslims, such as the Habous quarter, were laid out in Casablanca to the design of French architects. Their external appearance was of traditional, walled towns, while the domestic layouts drew on the typology of courtyard gardens, fountains, and flexible living rooms (Cohen and Eleb 2002, 214–226; Cohen 2006; Eleb 2000; Falehat 2014). The intention was to provide habitat, including both housing and neighborhood structure, which was appropriate for the residents' social norms and religious practices, while the picturesque urban décor also served to support a growing touristic market for local color, supplementing the old casbah.

Scholars have also noted an imperialist and self-reflective agenda in this citation of traditional forms and spaces (Fuller 2008; Yacobi and Shadar 2014, 975–997). With the influence of modernist architectural ideas emphasizing simple stereometric forms, settlements like the casbah were revalued for their simple, cohesive cubic form, which were appropriated by French architects, both to house the *colons* (the European colonists, both French and other nationalities), and eventually for housing the "indigenous peoples"—Arabs, Berbers, and Jews. The architect of the Habous quarter, Albert Laprade, described the new style of Lyautey's projects as a "synthesis of our Latin spirit and love for autochthonous art" (Cohen and Eleb 2002, 150, cited in Fuller 2008, 978–979). This statement reflects a prevalent discourse of what has been described as "Mediterraneanism," in which a linkage was made to the ancient culture of Greece and Rome; the Arab village was regarded as a (primitive) descendent of this culture, of which the French were regarded as the inheritors. Through this mythologization of the Mediterranean, the recent history of the Ottoman Empire was elided (Fuller 2008, 984). Thus, cultural memory was fabricated on several levels, that of the Islamic, but also that of Jewish colonized subjects and of the colonizers.

In the post–Second World War period of economic expansion in French North Africa, and in response to the internal migration of "indigenous peoples," multidisciplinary teams of French architects and planners proposed that the discussion of mass dwelling should be undertaken under the rubric of "habitat," an organic and interconnected relationship between diverse urban activities and functions, rather than under that of "mass-housing" (Cohen and Eleb 2002, 325). This notion of "habitat," was probably first promulgated by the leading French architect, Le Corbusier, in relation to his Marseilles *Unité d'habitation* (1947–1952— Unity of Habitat); it was distinguished from the earlier modernist category of housing (Mumford 2000) and built on both geographers' studies of space and land-zoning and anthropologists' studies of the way in which certain social practices, both everyday and exceptional, evolved in relation to particular climatic and geographical contexts to produce cultural specificity. And yet the new term, "habitat," with its reference to a grounded culture, contained an inherent contradiction, given that the "progressive" architects of the *Congrès international d'architecture moderne* (CIAM— International Congress of Modern Architecture) were committed to universal standards of enlightened civilization. The design of culturally specific habitats was rather conceived of as a necessary bridging infrastructure for populations whose cultural development was deemed to be insufficient to successfully embrace the more advanced Western secular culture (Eleb 2000, 55ff).

The director of planning in French Morocco, Michel Écochard, proposed the provision of housing settlements for "indigenous peoples" based on the concept of what he termed "secular customs"; these were seen to consist of the secluded space of the family and clan, the gendered space of male–female interactions, and the pronounced cultural division between interiority and exteriority, together with the social spaces of the bazaar and mosque (Cohen and Eleb 1998, 332–335; Eleb 2000, 56–61). Écochard's policy of housing based on secular customs reflected the real cultural differences not just between Europeans and "indigenous peoples" but also between the largely Berber rural populations and the urbanized Arabs of the coastal cities. However, some of the behavioral and cultural norms constituting Écochard's secular customs, such as patterns of spatial use, ideas of privacy, and spatial hierarchies, crossed ethnic and religious boundaries, as Abu-Lughod has noted (1987, 161).

Under Écochard's guidelines, a predominantly horizontal housing layout—closer to a traditional village structure and scale—was felt appropriate for the most "socially backward" populations. The *ATBAT-Afrique* settlements, notably the *Carrières Centrales* designed by a team led by Candilis, under Écochard's direction (Avermaete 2005), featured shaded pedestrian streets and private courtyards onto which opened one to three optimally south-facing rooms, a typology that was thought to respond to the gendered space of traditional Arab and Berber Muslims, but also followed the French colonial model of a Mediterranean habitat (Écochard 1955 cited in Eleb 2000, 56). However, as stated above, this spatial structure was conceived of as a bridge between the "static" culture of traditional Islamic societies and the enlightened one of modern rational society (Eleb 2000, 59).[2] In 1953, this project was presented by Écochard and the co-designer, Candilis, to the Ninth Congress of CIAM at Aix-en-Provence, as an example of the new paradigm of "habitat," for which it formed a strong stimulus (Mumford 2000, 234). The paradigm fully emerged at the 1970–1976 Architectural Congresses in Iran, where leading international figures, including Écochard and Candilis, met to debate an appropriate habitat for that Islamic nation (Bakhtiar and Farhad 1970, 249–250).

Designing for Cultural Continuity: Shushtar No'w, Iran

Underpinning the new concept of "habitat" was both a dismissal of abstract planning structures, in which housing was seen to have been secondary to zoning diagrams, and a belief in the ability of the architectural form and space of social housing to provide the scaffolding for authentic forms of social life and community to develop. In the same period, authorities in developing countries, such as Iran, similarly grappled with the problem of how to create culturally authentic habitat in the face of similar problems of population displacement and housing shortages in the cities—the byproducts of processes of modernization.

The 1970s oil economy of Iran, and its associated rapid modernization, had the negative consequence of a population displacement from rural villages to larger industrial cities and towns (Mahdavy 1965). This, as Diba observed, fueled the growth of squatter housing and escalated socioeconomic problems (Safran 1980, 38). Faced with this crisis, the government initiated a centrally planned housing program that considered a range of potential solutions, including the importation of factory-made, prefabricated housing—a key topic of the 1970 First International Congress of Architects in Iran, held in Isfahan (Westbrook and Mozaffari 2015). In the following 1974 Congress in Persepolis, a motion was carried that the Iranian government should commission the design of model housing projects, embodying the new concept of "habitat." Of the subsequent government-funded model housing communities, the most paradigmatic project was the company housing complex Shushtar No'w (New Shushtar), near the historic city of Shushtar in Khuzestan. The commission was awarded in 1975, a year after the Persepolis Congress, to Kamran Diba's firm DAZ Architects, Planners, and Engineers (Shirazi 2013).[3] The outcome was one of the most celebrated and publicized examples of new town design in the developing world, as reflected in numerous journal publications, and its appearance on the cover of the 1990 volume of the Aga Khan Awards Foundation (Powell 1990). In 1986, it received an Aga Khan Commendation, the first-stage design having been approved by 1977, and completed in 1980, after Diba's departure from Iran.

The design for Shushtar No'w was based on an attempt to reinterpret the appearance and structure of traditional towns in the region, and specifically the ancient towns of Shushtar, and using narrow alleyways that would provide shade and habitable roofs to permit sleeping on the roofs during hot summer nights (Fig. 4.1).[4] The project was praised by the 1986 Aga Khan Award panel for its having remained "faithful to the tradition, customs, ambitions and needs of the people of a region through an architecture expressing these aspirations and engendering balance and harmony," for creating and facilitating a sense of community through its spatial network and for establishing a meaningful formal and spatial dialogue with the old city of Shushtar (Serageldin 1989, 165).

For the Aga Khan Awards panel, Shushtar No'w appeared as an intentionally unified cultural project that effected a continuity with traditional local vernacular architecture through its materiality and spatial network. The jury chairman noted the need to deal, in such projects, with "the special values of traditional societies" (Serageldin 1989, 69). This is similar to the call in the 1974 Persepolis Architects Conference—at which Écochard and Candilis were both invited delegates—for the creation of housing that responds to the desirable diversity of perceptions and means inherent in "the shaping of the human habitat in time and place" (Bakhtiar 1974, 360). Indeed, in many respects the design *is* responsive to its local

Fig. 4.1 A pedestrian walkway in Shushtar No'w, development stage 1 (Photograph by Ali Mozaffari, 1993)

context. Thus, rather than following the modern functional program of a house, the layout of apartments is derived from spatial units of rooms which are all of a larger-than-typical size; this permits functional flexibility, akin to the traditional diurnal and seasonal variations in spatial use within the house, as well as consisting of two zones separating private family area from external and socializing areas. Second, like the *ATBAT-Afrique* housing, there is a hierarchy of courtyards from individual, to community and urban scale. The brick walls and vaulted roofs and internally oriented openings shield against the harsh sunlight and privilege the courtyard garden, while providing a culturally appropriate social seclusion. Finally, the design was consciously based on a sociological study of the way in which people in nearby towns interacted in public and private space (Shirazi 2013, 36).

But the most noticeable aspect of the project is its citation of a lexicon of selected *images* of traditional architecture. The urban configuration is based, in Diba's words (1980, 4), on the concept of a fire temple courtyard occupying the highest part of the hill, and forming an axial center for two broad spines of open space at right angles to each other, thus forming a configuration similar to that of a traditional Persian garden, or *Chahar-Bagh* (fourfold garden). This indeed invokes aspects of cultural memory from various historical periods, asserting a common pattern of spatial culture for a considerable duration of time, presumably with the objective of preserving them as functional memory. In this regard, it can be argued that Diba's action is one of heritage preservation. In the original design, the axial spines were extensively landscaped as a series of shady garden rooms, while in each of the four resultant quadrants, narrow, shaded pedestrian streets connect to local neighborhood courtyards, or *maidanche*, and are abutted by blocks of courtyard houses separated by lanes stepping down the hill, recalling the traditional residential quarters, or *mahalleh*. While the design is undoubtedly influenced by the projects presented at the Iran Congresses, notably the North African housing, the built project conveys an image that resonates with its traditional context: Lattice-brickwork bridges frame the residential streets at points adjacent to neighborhood courtyards (Fig. 4.2), recalling similar details in the nearby town of Dezful where Diba had undertaken a master plan,[5] while the central pedestrian spine of the master plan is reminiscent of the Isfahan bazaar plan. The overall layout is a constructed image of unity.

The desired unity at New Shushtar was effected, we would argue, through the montaging of reassuring images, in support of a desired connection to traditional habitat. In this respect, it is proposed that, rather than constituting a continuity with tradition, the project is a product of modern techniques, in which aspects of traditional buildings and towns have been cited, while figures and images have been appropriated from Western sources, most evidently the subcontinental work of the widely influential American architect, Louis Kahn, who was a key figure at the 1970 Congress in Isfahan.[6] In an interview we conducted, Diba's former associate, Kashanijoo, noted that the intention was to design a "total environment," a notable theme of the Iran Congresses,[7] where in 1970, the Iranian-American architect, Nader Ardalan, supported by Kahn, had called for the conscious embrace of a unitary concept of culture in which material and spiritual worlds were in harmony (Bakhtiar and Farhad 1970, 31–44). This idea of an authentic culture found its image in the form of the traditional village or town, for which Isfahan served as a spectacular model. Indeed Diba, at the Third Aga Khan Congress in Jakarta,

Fig. 4.2 General view of Shushtar No'w rooftops, development stage 1 (Photograph by Ali Mozaffari, 1993)

characterized his own design for Shushtar No'w as maintaining a continuity with Iranian traditions in its construction and spatial structure (Safran 1980, 41–44). The model for such desired continuity was the traditional house, village, and city (Bakhtiar 1974, xvii).

Conclusion

The dynamic relationship between habitat and social space raises a significant question for discussions of a putative Islamic heritage. Might intentionally designed projects of local and "Islamic" architecture, through the habitualizing of particular spatial performances—or through repetition—constitute in time, both an "invented tradition" (Hobsbawm 1983) and, consequently, heritage? But perhaps the more pertinent question here is to ask, following Thomas (1992, 216), "against what are traditions invented?" In the context of this chapter, this Other—that which is not heritage—is the process of globalization and economic and demographic transformation allegorized as "Western culture," the symptoms of which are uneven development, displacement, and industrialization. In the discourse of the Aga Khan Awards symposia, the Other was seen to endanger a precious heritage, and in reaction to which the traditional city was incapable of adapting. Processes of globalization are therefore deeply implicated in both creating and questioning the notion of "Islamic Heritage."

As we have argued in this chapter, putative Islamic authenticity in architecture travels from housing projects for the "indigenous" in French colonial North Africa to the town of Shushtar No'w in Iran through a process whereby well-placed local actors—in our case, the Empress Farah Diba and the organizers of the Iranian Congresses of Architects, notably her cousin Kamran Diba—invited the participation of leading architects and planners to present their perspectives, which could lead to collaborations on model projects. As outlined earlier, one such example of a model project was Shushtar No'w. In turn, this project, which owed much to its colonial models, was embraced by the Aga Khan Foundation as a paradigmatic example of Islamic housing. This project drew on the heritage of existing towns, creating familiar memories through the assemblage of the "thick images" of decorative motifs, screening and shading structures, courtyard buildings, narrow pedestrian streets, and a simulated bazaar structure, through which a "continuity" with the Islamic heritage of Iran was attempted. This process worked on the ground since it remained unquestioned, and from the outside it was confirmed by the reception it received from proponents of Islamic identity and heritage.

Through its play of images and motifs, Shushtar No'w also served a didactic role; a substantial proportion of the intended residents were of nomadic origins who were being encouraged to settle and had little or no experience of urban or perhaps even village life. While they shared religious and social values with the local population, their encounter with the habitat of Shushtar No'w was one—as in North Africa—of acculturation where, we would argue, the construction of social memory was effectively attempted. For the new residents, perhaps, a form of communicative memory (the unofficial and quotidian) could be engendered through the repetitive activities and rituals of everyday (Erll 2011, 28). But can this processual memory be stated as evidence of an essential Islamic heritage and identity? We would argue that such identity has been ascribed to objects and spaces that have a syncretic formation. The discourse of "Islamic habitat" as exemplified by the Aga Khan Awards and Shushtar No'w in particular is connected to and paralleled by that of the Islamic city.

Both are linked to the same narratives of political Islam that would become dominant from the early 1980s. It may be true that the universalized idea of the Islamic city as such is a French (or in another narrative, American) Orientalist invention (Aldous 2013). But there is, so far, little that explains the currency of this invention beyond Western scholars and indeed among broad sectors of Muslim intelligentsia around the globe, in which the narrative of the Islamic city and its heritage are presented as a fait accompli. Such a rise in interest in Islamic heritage could reasonably be explained through globalizing processes. As scholars in the field have correctly observed, this interest is a symptom of, among other things, the intertwined projects of modernity and globalization (Anheier and Yudhishthir 2011; Appadurai 1996; Beck 2000; Tsing 2005). Heritage is a globalizing project (Harrison 2015), one which has been brought forth through the growing interconnectedness of various areas of politics, culture, and economy, together with various modes of circulation of things and ideas; it operates on the three arenas of politics, economy, and culture and is facilitated through travel and technological advancements such as communications.

The rising interest in the Islamic city, not as a museum, but as a living emplacement of cultural heritage, arises from this type of circulation of material (in this case, housing), people (those working in the colonies or even as contractors in the developing world), and ideas (the Islamic city itself)—a process of "design" that is globalizing, comprised of modern education and techniques, in which a dialogical relationship between the present and the past is constructed. However, in this increased exposure to the Other, and a consequent increase in multivocality and diversity, there has arguably developed a growing sense of discontinuity with the past, a rupture (following Appadurai and Harrison) that has heightened the significance of heritage, and has resulted in "a series of material and discursive interventions which actively remake the world in particular ways" (Harrison 2015, 297). The Islamic habitat and architecture discourse is but one such instance. Instead of creating uniformity, globalization also creates "frictions," from which arise various discourses of identity. Thus, for example, the moving feast of the Aga Khan Symposia (beginning incidentally in France) was itself part of this circulation and an attempt at creating an Islamic world.

But, as our examples in North Africa and Iran have suggested, the Islamic architecture discourse is also born of specific conditions on the ground: the movement of people resulting from processes of modernization; the type of material, as this too gives a certain look or experience; and the available technologies—hence the line of discussion about technology and tradition in the 1970s Iranian Congress series—which also determine what *can* be built. Through these contingencies, a processual social memory, and a similarly processual heritage result which, following Harrison, we would argue is the outcome of something akin to a design process, a fabrication, and is materialized on the ground as such (Harrison 2015). This product of "design" amounts to the heritage itself, the concretization of memory. From this perspective, it is possible to reconsider our example of Muslim habitat at Shushtar No'w, notwithstanding its evident syncretic basis, as drawing on both imagistic assemblages of traditional settlements and modern conceptions of mass housing, in order to constitute through its design a habitat in which certain cultural traits could be preserved and prolonged. This prolongation, the objective behind Diba's design, which he characterized as a project of cultural continuity, is, we would argue, a dialogue with the past through the medium of design in order to shape the present and can thus be defined as a modern heritage process. This thus raises the issue of whether Shushtar No'w and projects of its ilk are worthy of consideration for their heritage value, not because they are examples of Islamic heritage but because they are the heritage product of global processes.

Notes

1. The fabrication of a modern Islamic identity is beyond the focus of this chapter but is discussed, for example, in Enyat, *Modern Islamic Political Thought* and Mozaffari, *Forming National Identity in Iran: The Idea of Homeland Derived from Ancient Persian and Islamic Imaginations of Place.*
2. The architects working under Écochard were both French and native-born Moroccan and included Georges Candilis and Shadrach Woods, both of whom had worked for Le Corbusier on the *Unité d'habitation* at Marseilles (1947–1952) and were co-founders of *ATBAT-Afrique* in Casablanca. Écochard and Candilis would be influential delegates at the 1974 Persepolis Architectural Congress.
3. Kashanijoo, Ahmad. Interview by Ali Mozaffari. Online. November–December 2014. Noorheyhani, Hamid. Interview by Ali Mozaffari. Online. November–December 2014.
4. Kashanijoo, Ahmad. Interview by Ali Mozaffari. Online. November–December 2014. Noorheyhani, Hamid. Interview by Ali Mozaffari. Online. November–December 2014.

5. Kashanijoo, Ahmad. Interview by Ali Mozaffari. Online. November–December 2014. Noorheyhani, Hamid. Interview by Ali Mozaffari. Online. November–December 2014.
6. The Jewish American architect, Louis Kahn, was highly influential on the development of a discourse of Islamic architecture through his commissions in India and Bangladesh, notably the Indian School of Management at Ahmedabad, and the National Parliament complex at Sher-e-Bangla in Bangladesh. Notoriously, the latter building was denied an award by the inaugural Aga Khan awards panel, ostensibly because of its cultural distance from its constituency.
7. Kashanijoo, Ahmad. Interview by Ali Mozaffari. Online. November–December 2014. Noorkeyhani, Hamid. Interview by Ali Mozaffari. Online. November–December 2014.

Bibliography

Abu Lughod, Janet L. 1987. "The Islamic City: Historic Myth, Islamic Essence and Contemporary Relevance." *International Journal of Middle East Studies* no. 19 (2): 155–176.

Aldous, Gregory. 2013. "The Islamic City Critique: Revising the Narrative." *Journal of the Economic and Social History of the Orient* no. 56 (3): 471–493.

Anheier, Helmut K., and Raj Isar Yudhishthir 2011. *Cultures and Globalization: Heritage, Memory and Identity.* London: SAGE Publications.

Appadurai, Arjun. 1996. *Modernity at Large.* Minneapolis: University of Minnesota Press.

Assmann, Aleida. 2011a. *Cultural Memory and Western Civilization: Functions, Media, Archives.* Cambridge: Cambridge University Press.

Assmann, Jan. 2011b. "Communicative and Cultural Memory." In *Cultural Memories: The Geographical Point of View,* edited by Peter Meusburger, Michael Heffernan, and Edgar Wunder, 15–27. Heidelberg, Germany: Springer.

Avermaete, Tom. 2005. *Another Modern: The Post-War Architecture and Urbanism of Candilis-Josic-Woods.* Rotterdam, The Netherlands: Nai.

Bakhtiar, Laleh. 1974. *Towards a Quality of Life: The Role of Industrialization in the Architecture and Urban Planning of Developing Countries. Report of the Proceedings of the Second International Congress of Architects, Persepolis, Iran.* Tehran: Hamdami Foundation.

Bakhtiar, Laleh, and Leila Farhad 1970. *The Interaction between Tradition and Technology. Report of the Proceedings of the First International Congress of Architects, Isfahan, Iran.* Tehran, Iran: Ministry of Housing and Urban Development.

Beck, Ulrich. 2000. *What Is Globalization?.* Cambridge: Polity.

Cohen, Jean-Louis. 2006. "Architectural History and the Colonial Question: Casablanca, Algiers and Beyond." *Architectural History* no. 49: 349–372.

Cohen, Jean-Louis, and Monique Eleb 1998. *Casablanca: Mythes et Figures d'une Aventure Urbaine*. Paris: Hazan.
Cohen, Jean-Louis, and Monique Eleb 2002. *Casablanca: Colonial Myths and Architectural Ventures*. New York: Monacelli Press.
Diba, Darab. 1980. Architect's Design Report: Aga Khan Technical Review Summary. Philadelphia, PA: Aga Khan Award for Architecture 1986.
Dorraj, Manochehr. 1999. "The Crisis of Modernity and Religious Revivalism: A Comparative Study of Islamic Fundamentalism, Jewish Fundamentalism and Liberation Theology." *Social Compass* no. 46 (2): 225–240.
Écochard, Michel. 1955. 'Habitat musulman au Maroc,' L'Architecture d'Aujourd'hui 60: 36–40.
Eleb, Monique. 2000. "An Alternative to Functionalist Universalism: Écochard, Candilis, and ATBAT-Afrique." In *Anxious Modernisms: Experimentation in Postwar Architectural Culture*, edited by Sarah Williams Goldhagen and Rejean Legault. Cambridge, MA: Massachusetts Institute of Technology Press.
Erll, Astrid. 2011. *Memory in Culture*. Hampshire, UK: Palgrave Macmillan.
Falehat, Somaiyeh. 2014. "Context-Based Conceptions in Urban Morphology: Hezar-Too, an Original Urban Logic?" *Cities* no. 36: 50–57.
Fuller, Mia. 2008. "Mediterraneanism: French and Italian Architects—Designs in 1930s North Africa Cities." In *The City in the Islamic World*, edited by Renata Holod Salma, Khadra Jayyusi, Attilio Petruccioli, and André Raymond. Leiden, Netherlands: Brill.
Hanson, Brad. 1983. "The 'Westoxication' of Iran: Depictions and Reactions of Behrangi, Al-E Ahmad and Shari Ati'." *International Journal of Middle East Studies* no. 15 (1): 1–23.
Harrison, Rodney. 2015. "Heritage and Globalization." In *The Palgrave Handbook of Contemporary Heritage Research*, edited by Emma Waterton and Steve Watson, 297–312. Basingstoke, Hants, UK: Palgrave Macmillan.
Hobsbawm, Eric. 1983. "Introduction: Inventing Traditions." In *The Invention of Tradition*, edited by Eric Hobsbawm and Terence Ranger, 1–14. Cambridge: Cambridge University Press.
Holod, Renata. 1980. *Toward an Architecture in the Spirit of Islam, Proceedings of Seminar One, Architectural Transformations in the Islamic World, Aiglemont, Gouvieux, France, April 1978*. Philadelphia, PA: Aga Khan Awards.
Juergensmeyer, Mark. 1993. *The New Cold War? Religious Nationalism Confronts the Secular State*. Berkeley: University of California Press.
Mahdavy, Hossein. 1965. "The Coming Crisis in Iran." *Foreign Affairs*.
Mozaffari, Ali. 2014. *World Heritage in Iran: Perspectives on Pasargadae*. Farnham, Surrey, UK: Ashgate.
Mumford, Eric 2000. *The CIAM Discourse on Urbanism*. Cambridge, MA: Massachusetts Institute of Technology Press.

Thomas, Nicholas. 1992. 'The inversion of tradition', *American Ethnologist* no. 19 (2) May: 213–232.

Nora, Pierre 1989. "Between Memory and History: Les Lieux de Mémoire." *Representations, Special Issue: Memory and Counter-memory* no. 26: 7–24.

Otto, Ton, and Poul Pedersen 2005. *Tradition and Agency: Tracing Cultural Continuity and Invention.* Aarhus: Aarhus University Press.

Powell, Robert 1990. *The Architecture of Housing.* Singapore: Concept Media, The Aga Khan Award for Architecture.

Rabinow, Paul. 1989. *French Modern: Norm and Forms of Social Environment.* Cambridge, MA: MIT Press.

Safran, Linda. 1980. "Housing Process and Physical Form." In *Housing Process and Physical Form, Proceedings of Seminar Three, Architectural Transformations in the Islamic World, Jakarta, Indonesia,* edited by Linda Safran, *March 26–29, 1979.* Philadelphia, PA: Smith, Edwards, Dunlop.

Serageldin, Ismail. 1989. *Space for Freedom: The Search for Architectural Excellence in Muslim Societies.* London: The Aga Khan Award for Architecture, Butterworth Architecture.

Shirazi, Reza M. 2013. "From 'Shustar No' to 'Shahre Javan Community'." *Young Cities Research Paper Series, T.U. Berlin* no. 7.

Tsing, Anna. 2005. *Friction: An Ethnography of Global Connection.* Princeton, NJ: Princeton University Press.

Westbrook, Nigel, and Ali Mozaffari. 2015. A Return to the Beginnings of Regionalism: Shushtar New Town Seen in the Light of the 2nd International Congress of Architects, Persepolis, Iran 1974. Paper read at SAHANZ: Architecture, Institutions and Change—Proceedings of the Society of Architectural Historians, Australia and New Zealand, 7–10 July at Sydney.

Yacobi, Haim, and Hadas Shadar 2014. "The Arab Village: A Genealogy of (Post) colonial Imagination." *The Journal of Architecture* no. 19 (6): 975–997.

Ali Mozaffari is research fellow at Alfred Deakin Institute, Deakin University and adjunct research fellow at the Australia-Asia-Pacific Institute, Curtin University, Australia. He is the founding coeditor of the book series *Explorations in Heritage Studies* (Berghahn) and author of *World Heritage in Iran; Perspectives on Pasargadae* (Routledge 2016).

Nigel Westbrook is associate professor and associate dean (Research) at the University of Western Australia, lecturing in the areas of architecture and urban design, architectural history, and urban studies. His research interests include the sixteenth-century Lorichs panorama of Istanbul, the Byzantine Great Palace and its urban context in Constantinople, and modern Iranian architecture.

Open Access This book is licensed under the terms of the Creative Commons Attribution 4.0 International License (http://creativecommons.org/licenses/by/4.0/), which permits use, sharing, adaptation, distribution and reproduction in any medium or format, as long as you give appropriate credit to the original author(s) and the source, provide a link to the Creative Commons license and indicate if changes were made.

The images or other third party material in this chapter are included in the chapter's Creative Commons license, unless indicated otherwise in a credit line to the material. If material is not included in the chapter's Creative Commons license and your intended use is not permitted by statutory regulation or exceeds the permitted use, you will need to obtain permission directly from the copyright holder.

CHAPTER 5

Framing the Primordial: Islamic Heritage and Saudi Arabia

Ömer Can Aksoy

Abstract This chapter addresses the concept of "Islamic Heritage" from the perspective of the theological questions on the primordial status of Islam, considering the interpretation of the concept of *fitra* in Muslim scholarship, particularly those raised by Salafi scholars. I argue that it is atypical to frame any period of the past as Islamic within the setting of Muslim World, since Islam regards itself as the primordial faith. I refer to two case studies from Saudi Arabia where the Muhammad ibn Abd-al-Wahhab's movement has had a significant impact on both an official historiography and the heritage management of the Kingdom: Saudi Arabian museums and the Hejaz Railway, which demonstrate the ways in which different epochs of the past in Saudi Arabia are made to conform to a specific Islamic timeline.

Keywords Islamic Archaeology · rock art · museums · the Hejaz Railway · Ottoman · Saudi Arabia

INTRODUCTION

This chapter scrutinizes the concept of "Islamic heritage" from the perspective of theological questions on the primordial status of Islam. My argument rests on the assertion that it is atypical to frame any period of the past as

Ö. C. Aksoy (✉)
UCL Qatar, Doha, Qatar

© The Author(s) 2017
T. Rico (ed.), *The Making of Islamic Heritage*, Heritage Studies in the Muslim World, DOI 10.1007/978-981-10-4071-9_5

Islamic within the context of the Muslim world, since Islam regards itself as the primordial faith. In order to demonstrate this claim, I focus on case studies from Saudi Arabia where Muhammad ibn Abd-al-Wahhab's movement has a considerable foothold in both an official historiography and the heritage management of the Kingdom. Consequently, in this chapter I revisit the interpretations concerning the concept of *fitra* (the primordial state of humankind) in Muslim scholarship, particularly those raised by Salafi scholars. Under the light of this theological background, this chapter presents fieldwork in Saudi Arabian museums and on the Hejaz Railway.[1] Both of these case studies illustrate the ways that different periods of the past in Saudi Arabia are made to conform to a specific Islamic timeline.

In the academic sense, the word "Islamic" is a qualifier that can be applied to describe a wide range of disciplinary foci, including but not limited to architecture, archaeology, and heritage (Grube 1978; Insoll 1999, 2007; Milwright 2010, 11). However, it is worth noting that, generally speaking, the disciplines of Islamic archaeology and Islamic architecture are dominated by a secular viewpoint; therefore, questions about the origin and scope of Islam have largely been avoided in these disciplinary frameworks. Rather, various "key points" have been formalized in order to identify the material culture of Islam in archaeological and architectural contexts (see Grube 1978; Milwright 2010, 125–158; Petersen 1996, 2014). For instance, Petersen (2014) counts mosques, the hajj routes, shrines, and the halal diet as areas of research that are of particular significance to an understanding of Islam. In contrast, Insoll (1999, 2007) casts a more inclusive role for Islamic archaeology in consideration of the potential influence of Islam on all aspects of Muslims' lives. He suggests that an archaeology of Islam "must be regarded as a complete system," a "residue" of individuals and beliefs spread over time and space (Insoll 1999, 228). Such a research approach can cover the cultural diversity and human agency in Muslim communities of the past in a more holistic way, but it has nonetheless failed to address a holistic manifestation of faith in that it rules out the concepts of *fitra*, *qadar* (pre-destination), and *dalal* (going astray) in Islam. Muslim scholars have fiercely debated the relationship between these concepts for centuries. These arguments rest particularly on the question of whether divine knowledge predetermines human choice on matters of faith and beliefs (Holtzman 2010, 176–177). I believe these arguments are vital to comprehend the approaches of Muslim polities and individuals to the past, the practice of archaeology, and heritage management. The naming of the

Nabatean settlement of Hegra (al-Hijr) as Mada'in Saleh, or cities of Saleh in reference to Prophet Saleh, is case in point (Nehmé 2007, 12). The verses about al-Hijr and Prophet Saleh in the Qur'an point out a case where a community (the Thamud) acted against the will of God (by slaying of she-camel), denied the messages of his messenger (Prophet Saleh), and faced the wrath of God as result of its act (see al-A'raf: 73–79; al-Hijr: 80). Eventually, Hegra came to be viewed as an unpleasant area in Muslim tradition and the present-day surrounding community (Alrawaibah 2013, 149). A comprehensive definition of these concepts is beyond the scope of this example and the present chapter (see Holtzman 2010, 167–172); I will therefore focus on the concept of *fitra* since, I suggest, it plays a key role in the heritage management of Saudi Arabia.

Primordial Time

The notion of *fitra* in the Qur'an (Surat al-Rum, verse 30) and various hadiths of Bukhari and Muslim enrich as well as complicate our understanding of the sense of the past in Islam and among Muslims. There are several meanings attested to the term *fitra* by a number of scholars: the state of Islam (Ibn Taymiyya), the natural union with Allah (Ibn Abd al-Wahhab), and the state of perfection (Ibn Abd al-Barr). Two conflicting views can be drawn from these explanations. One of these suggests that the concept of *fitra* addresses the belief that the sense of Allah and Islam exists in all human beings at the time of their birth. This view was mainly adopted by Ibn Taymiyya and Ibn Abd al-Wahhab. They considered that the inclination toward any other beliefs in a lifetime is a diversion from human nature (Ibn Abd Al-Wahhab 2010, 43–92; Holtzman 2010, 167–181; Hökelekli 1996, 47–48; Noyes 2013). The second view, which was raised by Ibn Abd al-Barr, puts forward the belief that all human beings are born in a neutral state, but with the potential to embrace Islam (Adang 2000, 408; Hökelekli 1996, 47–48).

Given the tenor of these interpretations, all pasts, including one's personal past, can be labeled as Islamic. The concept of *fitra* raises the question of whether to apply the term "Islamic heritage" to a period starting from 610 AD until this day or to refer to a timeline that reiterates this primordial principle. This question does not pose a major problem from the outlook of Islamic archaeology, since scholars draw lines in accordance with each period and type of material culture in their studies (Milwright 2010, 11–30; Petersen 2014, 6275). However, this is not merely a theological question that has implications for chronologies; it also directly addresses the complex relationship between present-day societies and the tangible and intangible heritage that is associated with Islam. Saudi Arabia exemplifies this challenge, where Ibn Abd al-Wahhab's ideals affect the official historiography of the Kingdom. In this discussion, I will address two case studies from Saudi Arabia: The first includes three museums, Tayma, al-Ula, and the National Museum, and the second examines the Hejaz Railway. These sites address two aspects associated with the categorization and problematization of the idea of an Islamic heritage and Islamic past. An examination of museums is aimed at the question of representation of pre- and post-seventh-century AD epochs, considering national and local museum narratives. These museums present Saudi Arabia's heritage in a primordial timeline that makes reference to the Qur'an, the official historiography, and to archaeological studies. An examination of the Hejaz Railway is aimed at scrutinizing the different meanings and labels that are attached to the Ottoman past by local populations and government bodies. In this case study, the concepts of Islamic heritage and Islamic past are critiqued through an analysis of one of the features that is presented as a defining element of the Railway: a hajj route (see Petersen 2014). The formation processes of the stations of this early-twentieth-century hajj route illustrate precisely how the terms "Islamic heritage" and "Islamic past" are loosely defined. My motivation for citing these two seemingly far-flung case studies is twofold. First, to illustrate that the concepts of "Islamic archaeology," "Islamic heritage," and "Islamic past" are in a state of flux. Though this has been argued by Millwright (2009, 2010) in relation to archaeological theory and methodologies and textual histories, this chapter offers a theological and historical basis for this argument. Second, to highlight the potential drawbacks in any attempt to contextualize the terms "Islamic archaeology," "Islamic heritage," and "Islamic past."

Museums of Messages

Saudi Arabia curates its history with respect to the Qur'an, traditional Muslim historiography, and archaeological research. This complex justification for curation manifests itself clearly in the designed spaces of the National Museum and the local museums of the Kingdom, creating a recognizable style. For example, the museums in al-Ula and Tayma are almost identical in terms of architecture and exhibition design. There are only differences between them regarding the contexts of the objects that are on display (see Michael Rice & Company Ltd. 1984). Boards, inscribed with Surat al-Rum's verse 9, are placed in the reception halls of these museums. The al-Ula and Tayma museums are not exceptional examples, as the Saudi Commission for Tourism and National Heritage (SCTH)[2] Museums Directory website stresses that Qur'anic verses are also on display in the entrance halls of Tabuk, Ha'il, and al Baha museums, though their verse numbers are not specified (SCTH 2014). These verses are described as "Qur'anic verses describing religion's relationship with archaeological studies" (SCTH 2014). That is to say, these boards contextualize archaeology and the museums in the realm of Islam—a vital prerequisite within the theocratic framework of the Saudi state and ulama (Commins 2006; *The Basic Law of Governance* 1992).

A closer look at verse 9 of the Surat al-Rum on the walls of al-Ula and Tayma museums deepens our understanding of the relationship between archaeology, Islam, and museums in Saudi Arabia:

> Have they not travelled in the land and seen what resulted in the end for those before them? They were more powerful than these, and they dug the earth, and built upon it more these have built. Messengers of their own came to them with clear proofs. God did not wrong them, but they did wrong themselves.
> (Surat al-Rum, verse 9: translation on the Tayma Museum's Board 2014)

Surat al-Rum plays a significant role in the debates on the concept of *fitra* among Muslim scholars, including Ibn Taymiyyah and Ibn Abd al-Barr (Hökelekli 1996, 47–48). In the view of these discussions, I suggest that the verse 9 boards in the entrance halls summon the visitors to question their own *fitra* while viewing the objects on display. Put in stark terms, these are didactic museums—museums of messages.

The National Museum highlights this primordial timeline to its visitors in greater detail than the Al-Ula and Tayma museums (see Okruhlik 2004, 213–215). The museum lies in the middle section of the King Abdul-Aziz Historical Center in Riyadh, which was founded to be "a cultural and civilization center highlighting the prominent history of the Arabian Peninsula and its historical message of disseminating Islam" (*Introduction, The National Museum* 2015). Both the architectural vocabulary and the narratives of the museum draw a "framework of geographical and cultural unity" (*Introduction, The National Museum* 2015) in order to create "a sense of continuity and dignity for all Saudis"

(Boddy 1999, 24). Artifacts, architectural finds, and replicas in this museum are displayed in seven sequential exhibition halls organized under the following themes:

1. "Man and Universe": origins of the Universe, geology, fossils, and Neolithic artefacts.
2. "The Arab Kingdoms": Arabian scripts and late Bronze Age—third century AD polities.
3. "*Al-Jahiliyyah* (Pre-Islamic) Era": caravan routes, markets, Arab poetry, and oasis settlements.
4. "The Prophet's Mission": the life of Prophet Muhammad, his lineage, and major events from his birth in Mecca until the *hijra* (the migration of the Prophet and his followers from Mecca to Medina) in 622 AD.
5. "Islam and the Arabian Peninsula": Umayyad-Abbasid, Mamluk, and Ottoman era finds, and Mecca.
6. "The First Saudi State and the Second Saudi State": the lives of Imam Muhammad bin Saud and Sheikh Mohammed bin Abdul Wahhab, and the history of Dirriyah.
7. "Unification of the Kingdom": the Unification War and King Abdulaziz's life.
8. "Hajj and the Two Holy Mosques": the role of previous polities in preserving the hajj rituals, historical hajj routes, the development of Mecca and Medina, and the role of the Saudi state in providing services to pilgrims.

The Qur'an has a significant role in the historical narratives of the National Museum in line with what is observed in the aforementioned local museum examples. The first thing that visitors encounter in the "Man and Universe" hall is a video installation featuring the universe under the title, "The Glory of His Creation." The board underneath the installation cites Al-A'raf, verse 54:

> Your Guardian-Lord is Allah, who created the heavens and the earth in six Days, and is firmly established on the Throne (of authority): He draweth the night as a veil o'er the day, each seeking the other in rapid succession: He created the sun, the moon, and the stars, (all) governed by laws under his Command. Is it not His to create and to govern? Blessed be Allah the Cherisher and Sustainer of the Worlds! (Yusuf 2000, 120, [*sic*])

The reason behind this installation becomes obvious when we take a closer look at the SCTH's webpage on the National Museum: "This hall reviews the scientific phenomena which shows the greatness of the Almighty Creator in the creation of the universe" (SCTH 2011). The impact of the Qur'an and the hadiths is less apparent in the "Arab Kingdoms" hall; the information presented in this hall is heavily reliant on the past three decade's excavation and survey results from northwestern Arabia. Nevertheless, a reference to the Surat al-Hijr is made in the museum guidebook on the foundation of the Mada'in Saleh (al Ghabban et al. 2011, 66).

The voice of traditional Muslim historiography takes the lead in the following "Pre-Islamic Era" exhibition hall. On the information board, the origin of Ka'ba is explained through al-Bakarah's verse 127 and al-Hajj's verse 26. Moreover, the hall's guidebook underlines the idolatry and polytheistic religions of this epoch from the traditional historiography's perspective:

> The god to whom be ascribed all perfection and majesty created the man as a monotheist for his god and worshiper to him naturally, but with the passing of time he goes far from monotheism and subjacent with myths" and "it's being believed that, verily Arabs still on religion of Ibrahim Al-Khalil (SAV) unto passing of two centuries on death of his son Ismail (SAV) then they started aberrancy towards myths and idolatry. (Al-Haffy 2007, 17, [sic])

These quotations recall the concept of *fitra* in Islam and explain why the pre-Islamic period is defined as *al-jahiliyyah* in the museum. This term, *al-jahiliyyah*, is derived from the word *jahl*, which means ignorance and passion. This "ignorance," implied in the hall guide, is neither artistic nor technological one but religious. In both the National Museum and the local museums, elements of this period are not labeled except using the concept of ignorance (Michael Rice & Company Ltd 1984; Zarins 1984). The complexity of settlements, markets, trade, and industry during the *al-jahiliyyah* era is stressed comprehensively throughout the National Museum. Above all, *al-jahiliyyah* poetry is praised and considered a significant component of the Kingdom's heritage. For instance, a poetry recital competition was held in the "*Al-Jahiliyyah* Era" hall on February of 2015, during which female students from public and private elementary schools wore "pre-Islamic era costumes" and recited pre-Islamic poems about the architectural model of Okaz Market in the hall (The National Museum 2015). Can the term *al-jahiliyyah* be discussed as a terminus ante quem for a definition of an Islamic past? The ongoing academic debates on the meaning of *al-jahiliyyah* and the broader application of this term in the Muslim historiography prove that it is an analytically loose term (Fayda 1993, 17–19; Webb 2014, 91–93).

A wide range of connotations have been ascribed to *al-jahiliyyah* since the ninth century AD. Some of the hadith collections, the Qur'an commentaries, and classical Arabic texts associate *al-jahiliyyah* with individualized pre-Islamic pasts of the first generation of Muslims, the heroism and nobility of Arab tribes, and a moral state of being without any reference to a time period. *Al-jahiliyyah* became a paradigmatic element for defining barbarism and idolatry in the late sources and was used for defining a pre-Islamic past and, in some cases, an apocalyptic future (Webb 2014, 70–75). Saudi historiography demonstrates these various connotations explicitly. The takfirist approach in Saudi historiography views "the age of ignorance" as encompassing not only the pre-Islamic era, but the entire period prior to the rise of Salafism.[3] On the other hand, some Saudi scholars, in particular al-Uthaymin and al-Ansary, link the use of the term "pre-Islamic civilization" with "unification of the kingdom" in the narratives of the National Museum. According to Matthias Determann (2014, 124–128), this debate reverberated in the exhibition narratives of the National Museum through the mixture of the results of archaeological research with elements of traditional Muslim historiography.

Nonetheless, with its circular atrium and long corridor, the "Prophet's Mission" hall constitutes an architectural watershed in the primordial timeline of the museum. Various manuscripts of the Qur'an are on display in the heart of the circular atrium lighted with layers of bright colors. Duskily lit, this long corridor—decorated with ceramic murals featuring the Prophet's migration to Medina—directs visitors to the next hall, "Islam and the Arabian Peninsula." The polities that emerged in the peninsula after the death of the Prophet are represented in this hall. A significant point to note in this hall is that the Ottoman period is presented alongside those of the Umayyads, Abbasids, and Mamluks. Adducing from the contents of the National Museum guidebook and the hall's guide, it is safe to suggest that the Ottoman past is considered an epoch of the Islamic era in the peninsula by the SCTH (see al-Gahbban et al. 2011). This epoch is mainly described with references to the proliferation of Ottoman defensive architecture in the peninsula and the expansion of Ottoman control from Hejaz to al-Hasa.

The two halls that follow in the museum focus on the first and the second Saudi states and the Unification War, featuring some elements of both the takfirist and unionist approaches to history. The museum guidebook states that "the first Saudi state promoted the law of God and the Sunnah of his Messenger" against "the heresies and superstitions that were widespread in the Najd at that time" (al Ghabban et al. 2011, 33). Moreover, King Abdulaziz's expeditions to Southern Najd, al-Qassim, the Hejaz, the Eastern Province, the Asir, Ha'il, Jazzan, and Tihamanah between 1903 and 1930 were not interpreted as jihad or Islamic conquests but as a quest for unity and stability (Al-Eissa 2007, 4–20; Determann 2014, 127). Last, the "Gallery of Hajj and the Two Holy Mosques" extends the scope of the theme of unity and stability to the global scale, by pointing out the Saudi Kings' title: the Custodian of the Two Holy Mosques (Al-Hadlaq 2007).

To summarize, the narratives of the National Museum and the museums of Tayma and al-Ula illustrate a broader conceptualization of Islamic past and heritage beyond a particular period and geography. Indeed, this past mastering in enclosed spaces has national, global, and dynastic elements in it, but the religious historiography remains the overarching aspect (see Determann 2014). I argue that this overarching role and the Islamic perception of a primordial time problematizes the use of "Islamic" as a disciplinary qualifier, while defining tangible and intangible heritage institutionally nonetheless.

The Hejaz Railway

With a length of over 1,900 km extending from Damascus to Medina, the Hejaz Railway was one of the most ambitious projects of the late Ottoman Empire at the beginning of the twentieth century. As a new hajj route made of steel and well-cut stone structures, the Hejaz Railway weakened the role of camel caravans in the hajj. The construction of the main line was launched in 1900 and finished in 1908 (Çetin 2010, 100–102; Hulagü 2008). The additional lines were built up until 1918. Station buildings, military outposts, telegraph lines, trenches, rails, and water wells were painstakingly set on the formidable desert and mountainous landscape during this period.

The construction of the Railway was financed through numerous sources: credits from the Ottoman Agricultural Bank; the sale of transaction stamps; donations from Muslim, Christian, and Jewish Ottoman citizens; as well as voluntary salary cuts among government officials. In particular, donations from the international Muslim community were pivotal both in terms of project feasibility and the Pan-Islamic agenda of Sultan Abdulhamid II. Their donations covered the expenditure for one-third of the construction project (Çetin 2010, 103–117; Hulagü 2008, 118–122; Koloğlu 2017, 242). These donations were a result of a well-conducted Ottoman propaganda campaign targeting both the Ottoman population and the international Muslim community. The construction project was publicized as a great project that would ease the travel of pilgrims to Mecca and Medina and "beatify the soul of the prophet and overwhelm the World Muslim population's blessings" (Çetin 2010, 101). Moreover, it was also promoted as a national financial investment in distant parts of the Empire (Çetin 2010, 103–105).

The Ottoman Empire's propaganda was well received in most of its provinces and among the international Muslim community, but it failed miserably in the Hejaz. One of the major reasons of this failure was the militaristic potential of the line. The fast and efficient transportation of Ottoman troops to the Hejaz was posing a significant threat to the de facto autonomy of the local tribes. Moreover, there were also economic reasons behind the local upheaval: The construction of the line meant a substantial decrease in the hajj transportation revenues of the local inhabitants. The Ottoman officials tried to convince the local inhabitants that the Railway would open a new corridor of trade for their products, such as wool and leather. However, these promises did not have a major resonance among local populations (Ozyuksel 2014, 86–160; Koloğlu 2017, 237–238). With the revolt of Sharif Hussein against the Ottoman Empire in 1916, the Pan-Islamic image of the Railway faded away. The carriages were now carrying soldiers, equipment, and provisions to the Hejaz. Consequently, the train line fell under the administration of the Military Railways and Ports Directorate in 1917 (Çetin 2010, 113). As an irony of fate, the trains of the Hejaz Railway carried away the artifacts housed in al-Masjid al-Nabawi (the Prophet's Mosque) to Istanbul during the siege of Medina in 1917. Nowadays, these artifacts constitute a substantial part of the "Sacred Relics Collection" of the Topkapı Palace (Bardakçi 2012; Nizamoglu 2013; Koloğlu 2017, 316).

Given its history, the Hejaz Railway could be viewed as Islamic heritage and an expression of faith, or as an expression of Ottoman control from Islamic archaeology's point of view. For my part, the

Hejaz Railway is an exemplary case that shows how problematic it can be to label a site as Islamic or not: While the takfirist paradigm in Saudi historiography associates the Ottomans with the notion of *al-jahiliyyah* (Determann 2014, 28), the Hejaz Railway is related to Pan-Islamism by various Turkish scholars (Çetin 2010, 103–117). Beyond these dichotomies, the material remains of the Railway and its surroundings bear witness to varying perceptions about this piece of Ottoman past lying on Saudi soil. Among these structures, the Railway's stations in Mada'in Saleh, al-Ula, Medina, and Tabuk stand as sites that have been altered, utilized, redefined, and recreated by both the local populations and the post-Ottoman polities of the region from their time of construction up to the present. In the following sections, a selection of these activities will be addressed in order to provide insight on the formation processes of the Hejaz Railway's material culture as well as the changing views pertaining to it.

Re-purposing an Ottoman Past

Starting with the Mamluk campaign of Sultan Selim I in 1516–1517, Ottoman claims and rule in the Hejaz took form mainly through large-scale construction projects. The Hejaz Railway was the final ring on a chain of imperial projects. In contrast with these imperial projects, rock art stands out as one of the major nonstate expressions of human presence in the Hejaz region. The walls of the Tabuk railway station and the rock faces in the surrounding landscape of the Railway have long been subjected to this form of art. The Tabuk station is not an isolated example: Graffiti and drawings have also been identified by the Great Arab Revolt Project team in Wadi Rum in Jordan (Saunders and Faulkner 2010, 520). Rock art is a centuries-old activity in Arabia, which can be traced back to the Iron Age through epigraphy, and according to some researchers, to the Neolithic, in respect to the arguable stylistic comparisons observed (Khan 1993, 2000, 13, 2007; Olsen 2013). However, the contemporary and the twentieth-century rock art examples have not been studied in depth. They are usually viewed as acts of vandalism by the SCTH, since most of the recorded examples were chipped or painted over earlier examples of rock art (see Alrawaibah 2013, 153). For my part, the vandalism theme is not explanatory in these cases since the older examples of rock art are usually applied on top of each other. The Tabuk station demonstrates a similar approach; a juxtaposition of state (station buildings) and nonstate (rock art) forms of expression.

A closer look at three wall drawings on the office-lodge building of the Tabuk station sheds light on the possible motives behind their application on its walls. A geometrical figure on one of the window niches of the Tabuk station building shows some close similarities with the *wusum* (tribal brands; singular *wasm*) of the al-Hatarsha and al-Shararat tribes from northern Saudi Arabia (see Dickson 1967; Field 1952; Khan 2000, 16–75). This particular mark might have been chipped by a member of a sub-tribe or branches of these tribes, since an additional mark was applied on the upper right-hand side of the figure. Presently, *wusum* are mainly used to brand livestock and personal objects like knives, rugs, and tents by tribe members in order to mark their ownership of commodities. In addition, *wusum* are well-known features of the rock art sites, particularly in the vicinity of key ground features such as wells, seasonal water ponds, and camp sites. It is not unusual to find the *wusum* of tribes in places far from their base. This suggests they are also signifiers of tribal and perhaps personal presence in a particular location.

Given the current state of evidence, whether the *wasm* in the Tabuk station is a sign of a commodity or a sign of presence is not clear. What is clear, however, is that this *wasm* is an expression of a local identity that stands in contrast with both the Pan-Islamic plans of Abdulhamid II and the later Ottomanist goals of the Young Turks in the Hejaz (Makdisi 2002, 768–771; Rogan 1996, 83–86). It is important to outline that the Tabuk station and the other stations in these rural areas were constantly targeted by Bedouin groups. Consequently, the Ottoman authorities replied to these attacks by fortifying the stations and their surrounding landscape and arming their train carriages (Hulagü 2008, 130; Ozyuksel 2014, 156; Saunders and Faulkner 2010, 519). To this end, the Railway became a symbol of otherness and oppression in the eyes of some of the paramount tribes such as the Bani Harb and Bani Ali (Nicholson 2005, 44–46; Ozyuksel 2014, 153–156). The Railway meant more centralized Ottoman control over the local tribes on crucial matters such as arms trade, hajj income, water supply, taxation, and conscription (Hulagü 2008, 127–128; Ozyuksel 2014, 219–225).

It is not possible to conclude whether the figures were applied to the walls while the Tabuk station was in use. Only a figure of a palm tree between two crossed sabers beside a windowsill can be dated to a particular period, since it is the national emblem of the Kingdom of Saudi Arabia since 1950 (Central Department of Statistics and Information 2015; Determann 2014, 9). In contrast with the *wasm* figure, the national emblem is one of the primary symbols of nation building in the present-day Saudi state, which emerged after a long war of unification between 1902 and 1932 (Al-Azzam et al. 2014, 31; Al-Simari 2012, 566; Leatherdale 1983, 37–45). An offshoot of the national emblem, such as the logo of SCTH, brings the unitarian intentions behind the national emblem to the forefront, representing how:

> [H]armonious lines of the logo converge to form a palm tree (a sign of generosity and hospitality) and a pair of crossing swords demonstrates authority, tradition and heritage. Thus, the logo reflects the singularity and the brevity of an official institution of a modern vibrant Saudi Arabia. Saudi Arabia with its different social customs, heritage and popular cultures in its regions is represented in the logo with thirteen acute angles of a palm. In fact, there are thirteen regions in the Kingdom with attractive tourism activities that are rich and unique. (SCTH 2015)

Presently, the SCTH logo is used on the information boards in the Tabuk station museum and on the signboard of the SCTH Tabuk branch, which is currently based in one of the station buildings. By doing so, the Tabuk station is rebranded as part of a common Saudi heritage by the SCTH.

Not all figures on the Tabuk station's office-lodge building are signifiers of a national or a tribal identity; some are simply a form of self-expression through art. Roughly rendered animal figures underneath one of the windowsills is a good example. The torso and the face of the animal are rectangular in shape and its legs, ears, and tail are rendered as straight lines. Given how it is drawn, the figure shares same stylistic characteristics with various equine and dog figures in the rock art sites across the Kingdom (see Khan 1993, 2007; Olsen 2013). The different contexts of these figures, ranging from the Ottoman railway structure to the pre-historic rock art site of Jubbah, indicate that the notions of style and identity have little value in proposing a chronology or an ideological framework for these figures. Perhaps, then, the flat slab stone might simply have been a suitable "canvas" for the application of this animal representation.

Utilizing and Refurbishing the Ottoman Past

Beyond its ideological and historical significance, the Hejaz Railway can be viewed as a complex structure comprised of iron rails and well-cut stone structures. These material remains of the Railway were reutilized by the local population in various ways up to the recent past. These activities can be dated back to the construction of the line; for instance, in 1908, the Ottoman officials reported that a large number of wooden telegraph poles and crossties were dismantled by the Bedouins. In response, the scraped crossties had to be replaced with steel ones (Ozyuksel 2014, 153). After the disbandment of the line, utilization of the Railway's construction materials by the locals became more complex. Some of the stations, such as the al-Ula station, were transformed into new and more confined spaces. The station buildings were enclosed by a mud-brick wall. Moreover, the interior became occupied by a series of mud-brick structures that were incorporated into the station buildings.

Observing photographs taken during the 1907 opening ceremony and the 1917 Hejaz Expedition, it is safe to assume that these additions were built after the station lost its original function (see Bragger 2002). In contrast with the late Ottoman and early-twentieth-century German-style buildings of the al-Ula station, the mud-brick structures manifest local architectural traits, such as saw tooth parapets and narrow wall slits (see Albini 1998). However, the roofing of these mud-brick structures was not made with traditional construction materials, such as palm trunks, but rather with iron rails dismantled from the Railway. A similar case can also be observed in the center of al-Ula town, where stone and mud-brick houses display the use of metal rails as door and window niches during.

As a result of government and private sector enterprises and projects in Saudi heritage tourism in the last two decades, the Hejaz Railway stations found themselves in the limelight (Burns 2007; Al Ghabban 2012). The sites started to be viewed as a touristic and cultural asset of the Kingdom at the official level. Some of the stations, including Medina, Mada'in Saleh, and Tabuk, were restored and refurbished under the supervision of SCTH. The Mada'in Saleh station was organized as a visitor center at the entrance of the Nabataean site of al-Hijr, which became Saudi Arabia's first World Heritage site in 2008 (Alrawaibah 2013). The visitor center comprises an exhibition hall, coffee shop, a projection room, toilets, and a bookshop. The relatively large and rectangular train maintenance workshops of Mada'in Saleh, Tabuk, and Medina stations are currently being used as exhibition halls. The reason behind this choice is quite obvious: The railway in the middle of the structure allows for the display carriages and trains to be under a roof, while the raised platforms around the railway offer an area for the display of information boards and artifacts in a linear way. In the case of Mada'in Saleh station, one of the carriages was transformed into a small screening room in which a documentary about the history of the line can be seen, attracting children in particular. Unlike the other stations, the Tabuk station is currently being incorporated into a contemporary piece of architecture to house the Tabuk Archaeology Museum. The museum is positioned behind the station buildings, and it will provide a larger exhibition area relative to the train maintenance workshops.

This interest in the Hejaz Railway is not just circumscribed to the circles of the SCTH; it is also raised by a number of independent scholars with different backgrounds (al Faqeer 2009, 174–182; Burns 2007, 227; Orbasli and Woodward 2008). For instance, Aylin Orbasli and Simon Woodward surveyed the entire railway line in Saudi Arabia between 2001 and 2004. They viewed the Railway and its associated structures as a cultural route stimulating heritage tourism in the country. In 2008, they proposed that the Railway line has a great potential to be a linear heritage attraction and "the physical remains of the Railway can be used as an anchor for the preservation and interpretation of the Islamic and pre-Islamic cultural heritage of the route" (Orbasli and Woodward 2008, 159). Dr. Bader Bin Adel Al Faqeer, associate professor in the Geography Department at King Saud University, looked at the Hejaz Railway from a more localized standpoint. In particular, he tackled the relationship between the components of the railway in al-Ula province and its surrounding landscape, considering picturesque views that the garrisons, stations, and railway tracks could offer to future visitors (al Faqeer, Badr Bin Adel Bin Mohammad 2009, 311–319). In this work, he describes the Hejaz Railway as "one of the most important archaeological monuments in Al-Ula province" (al Faqeer, Badr Bin Adel Bin Mohammad 2009, 311). This "importance" is explained through inclusion of the Hejaz Railway on the United Nations Educational, Scientific, and Cultural Organization's (UNESCO) tentative list and the site's potential as "a religious, cultural and strategic heritage" (al Faqeer, Badr Bin Adel Bin Mohammad 2009, 311; UNESCO 2015).

Exhibition and Revival of the Ottoman Past

Leaving aside the architectural changes made in these stations, a closer look at the information boards in the exhibition halls of the Mada'in Saleh and Tabuk stations offers a glimpse of the present-day official interpretation of the Hejaz Railway. Generally speaking, the boards describe the architectural features and the history of the Railway using a technical and a descriptive tone. However, beyond a conventional historical description of the Railway, there was a patron behind the Hejaz Railway project—Sultan Abdulhamid II, a historical figure who remains controversial today. As a result of his relatively oppressive rule, isolated life style, informer network, bold projects, and global vision, the image of the sultan was a deeply polarizing one among his contemporaries, and continues to be so among present-day societies that once lived under Ottoman rule (see Sakaoglu 1999, 535–538). The labels attested to him by both his opponents and his supporters best express this polarization: "The Red Sultan" (Roubille 1900, 1), "The Owl of the Yıldız Palace" (Ersoy 1999, 361), "The Accursed" (Ersoy 1999, 114), and "The Supreme Khan" (Fazıl 2007, 1). The exhibition boards in the Tabuk and Madain Saleh stations feature Abdulhamid II from a more positive angle by pointing out his plans to revive and modernize the Empire by the means of railways and telegraph lines. Yet, there is no mention of his Pan-Islamic agenda or his political plans for the region.

Alongside the aforementioned restoration and refurbishment activities, the Hejaz Railway has recently become an inspiration for a revivalist trend in Saudi architecture. The visitor center of Dedan, the Lihyanite capital, clearly illustrates this impact. The building shows some traits of the guard outposts on the railway line: well-cut stone walls, a triple-arched porch, and slightly rectangular layout. Yet the contemporary Saudi architectural elements can also be seen on this structure: Windows are longer and rectangular in form and they are coated with green film. This revivalist piece of architecture and its function as the visitor center of a pre–seventh-century AD site highlights the density of meanings and labels that can be ascribed to the Hejaz Railway. In this section, I tried to categorize these labels through fieldwork and literary survey. What these labels show us is an ongoing reinterpretation process. The Railway moved from being a project to "beatify the soul of the prophet" in 1900 (Çetin 2010, 101) to being a linear heritage attraction for today's tourists (see Orbasli and Woodward 2008). This sharp difference clearly illustrates that there is no single adjective, including Islamic, that can be used to label this railway system.

Conclusions

The discussion in this article suggests that "Islamic heritage" can only be defined as a highly subjective and problematic term. The case studies of Saudi museums and the Hejaz Railway recall the title of this chapter—"framing the primordial." They indicate a number of potential drawbacks for any attempt to contextualize terms such as "Islamic archaeology," "Islamic heritage," or "Islamic past." Taking a side in debates about faith is one of these major drawbacks. Islamic archaeology and emerging critical studies in Islamic heritage usually approach the material culture of different cultural and religious movements among Muslim societies and individuals from a secular tradition. This approach might be effective at avoiding a situation where Islamic archaeology is wielded as tool for questioning the validity of these faiths. However, this secular stance also takes a side in these debates by gathering different expressions of faith under the "Islamic" adjective. The description of the pre-Saudi period as *al-jahiliyyah* in the takfirist Saudi historiography, as well as ever-changing official and local perceptions concerning the Hejaz Railway, express the fluidity of the term "Islamic heritage." This fluidity pinpoints the second potential bias: the overlooking of any sociopolitical or personal connotations behind examples of tangible heritage. The formation processes of the Hejaz Railway structures, and the nationalist, global, and dynastical elements in the Saudi museums' narratives, can generate different adjectives depending on the outlook.

This point leads us to the final drawback: the vulgarization and fetishization of the "Islamic" adjective by attesting a certain material culture and timeframe to it. Generally speaking, the relationship between Muslims and a pre-Islamic past is presented as a case of apathy (see Blau 1995, 122; Liverani 2005, 225; Potts 1998, 195–196). The ambiguity of Muslims to a pre-Islamic past is expressed through few and overly repeated examples: Ibn al-Kalbi, al-Maqrizi, and Abd al-Latif's studies on the pre-Islamic past; revivalist demonstrations, like the 2,500 year celebration of the Persian Empire in 1971; and the admiration for *al-Jahiliyyah* poetry (see Hawting 1999, 2; Insoll 1999, 230; Milwright 2009, 5; Petersen 2014, 6269). The Saudi museums examined here suggest that a Muslim ambiguity to the pre-seventh-century AD period is beyond the scope of these fragmentary examples and references, at least on an official level. These museums manifest a primordial timeline within the contexts of Islam, official historiography, and archaeological studies. Above all, these case studies indicate that there is a much broader understanding of the Islamic past in regard to the Muslim belief that Islam is the primordial faith (Hawting 1999, 21; Kuzgun 1997; Leaman 2006, 242).

Notes

1. These sites were visited by the author in 2009, 2011, and 2014.
2. This name was adopted in 2015. The previous name of the organization was the Saudi Commission for Tourism and Antiquities (SCTA).
3. Saudi chronicler Husayn Ibn Ghannām framed the "takfīrist" paradigm (from *takfīr*, "to announce someone an unbeliever"). This paradigm argues that only the supporters of Ibn Abd al-Wahhab's mission, led by the Al Saud, were true Muslims (Determann 2012, 47).

Acknowledgments The author would first like to thank Dr. Trinidad Rico for encouraging him to present this paper at the Islamic Pasts workshop and for commenting on various drafts. The author would also like to thank Dr. Matthias Determann and Dr. Jose Carvajal Lopez for reading drafts of this paper and making many useful criticisms. Many thanks to Dr. Cemal Omer, Dr. Arnulf Hausleiter, Prof. Robert Carter, Prof. David Wengrow, Prof. Thilo Rehren, Alaa Alrawaibah, and Samovar Sami for their support in my field investigations.

Bibliography

Adang, Camilla. 2000. "Islam as the Inborn Religion of Mankind: The Concept of Fitra in the Works of Ibn Hamza." *Al-Qantara: Revista de Estudias Árabes* no. 21 (2): 390–409.

al Faqeer, Badr Bin Adel Bin Mohammad. 2009. *Nature and Antiquities in Al-Ula Province/Saudi Arabia a Touristic Jewel*. Riyadh, Saudi Arabia: King Fahd National Library.

Al Ghabban, Ali 2012. "Kingdom of Saudi Arabia and Its Heritage." In *Roads of Arabia: Archaeology and History of Kingdom of Saudi Arabia*, edited by Ali Al Ghabban, Béatrice André-Salvini, Françoise Demange, Carine Juvin, and M. Cotty, 35–39. Paris: Musée du Louvre.

al Ghabban, Ali, H.A. al-Hassan, al-Saud A., al-Ghazzi A., al-Salook M.A., al-Shammary J.B., al-Hadlaq A.S., al-Khalifa K., al-Badawi W., al-Hammad A., al-Baqia N., and M Khan. 2011. *The National Museum Guide*. Riyadh, Saudi Arabia: Saudi Commission for Tourism and Antiquities.

Al-Azzam, B., M Al-Ahaydib, and M Shalaby 2014. "The Socio-Cultural, Historical, and Political Allusions in the Translation of the Saudi National Day Poetry: 'Peace, O Gracious King' as a Case Study." *Studies in Literature and Language* no. 9 (3): 30–39.

Albini, Marco. 1998. *Traditional Architecture in Saudi Arabia: The Central Region*. Riyadh, Saudi Arabia: Ministry of Education, Kingdom of Saudi Arabia.

Al-Eissa, A.M. 2007. *Gallery of Unification of the Kingdom*. Riyadh, Saudi Arabia: National Museum.
Al-Hadlaq, A.S. 2007. *Gallery of Hajj and the Two Holy Mosques*. Riyadh, Saudi Arabia: National Museum.
Al-Haffy, M. 2007. *Gallery of the Pre-Islamic Era*. Riyadh, Saudi Arabia: National Museum.
Alrawaibah, Alaa. 2013. "Archaeological Site Management in the Kingdom of Saudi Arabia: Protection or Isolation." In *Cultural Heritage in the Arabian Peninsula: Debates, Discourses, and Practices*, edited by Karen Exell and Trinidad Rico, 143–156. Surrey, UK: Ashgate.
Al-Simari, F.A. 2012. "The Kingdom of Saudi Arabia." In *Roads of Arabia: Archaeology and History of Kingdom of Saudi Arabia*, edited by Ali Al Ghabban, Béatrice André-Salvini, Françoise Demange, Carine Juvin, and M. Cotty, 565–566. Paris: Musée du Louvre.
Bardakçi, Murat. *Kutsal Emanetler'deki Hazineler, Bugün Fahreddin Pasa'nın Sayesinde Bizdedir* 2012 [accessed August 5, 2015]. Available from http://www.haberturk.com/yazarlar/murat-bardakci/727818-kutsal-emanetlerdeki-hazineler-bugun-fahreddin-pasanin-sayesinde-bizdedir.
The Basic Law of Governance. Royal Embassy of Saudi Arabia, Washington, D.C. 1992 [accessed July 3, 2015]. Available from https://www.saudiembassy.net/about/country-information/laws/The_Basic_Law_Of_Governance.aspx.
Blau, Soren. 1995. "Observing the Present—Reflecting the Past. Attitudes Towards Archaeology in the United Arab Emirates." *Arabian Archaeology and Epigraphy* no. 6 (2): 116–128.
Boddy, Trevor. 1999. "History's New Home in Riyadh." *Saudi Aramco World* no. 50 (5): 22–29.
Bragger, Roger. *El Ula Station* 2002 [accessed August 10, 2015]. Available from http://www.rogersstudy.co.uk/hejaz/hejaz_railway/el_ula_station.html.
Burns, Peter. 2007. "From Hajj to Hedonism? Paradoxes of Developing Tourism in Saudi Arabia." In *Tourism in the Middle East: Continuity, Change, and Transformation*, edited by Rami F. Daher, 215–236. Clevedon, UK: Channel View Publications.
Central Department of Statistics and Information. 2015. *Facts about the Kingdom, Central Department of Statistics and Information*. Saudi Arabia: Central Department of Statistics and Information [accessed July 14, 2015].
Çetin, Emrah. 2010. "Türk Basinina Göre Hicaz Demiryolu." *History Studies, Middle East Special Issue*: 99–115.
Commins, David. 2006. *The Wahhabi Mission and Saudi Arabia*. New York: Palgrave Macmillan.
Determann, Jörg Matthias. 2012. *Globalization, the State and Narrative Plurality: Historiography in Saudi Arabia. Wusum*. London: Department of History, School of Oriental and African Studies.

Determann, Jörg Matthias. 2014. *Historiography in Saudi Arabia: Globalization and the State in the Middle East*. London: I.B. Tauris.
Dickson, Harold R.P. 1967. *The Arab of the Desert*. London: George Allen & Unwin Ltd.
Ersoy, Mehmet A. 1999. *Safahat*. Edited by M. Ertugrul Düzdag. Istanbul: Sule Yayinlari.
Fayda, Mustafa. 1993. "Cahiliye." *Türkiye Diyanet Vakfı Islam Ansiklopedisi* no. 7, 14–19.
Fazil, Necip F. 2007. *Ulu Hakan: Ikıncı Abdülhamid Han*. Istanbul: Büyük Dogu Yayınevi.
Field, Henry. 1952. "Camel Brands and Graffiti from Iraq, Syria, Jordan, Iran, and Arabia." *Journal of The American Oriental Society, Supplement 15*.
Grube, Ernst J. 1978. "What Is Islamic Architecture?" In *Architecture of the Islamic World: Its History and Social Meaning*, edited by George Mitchell, 10–15. New York: William Morrow and Company.
Hawting, Gerald R. 1999. *The Idea of Idolatry and the Emergence of Islam: From Polemic to History*. Cambridge: Cambridge University Press.
Hökelekli, Hayati. 1996. "Fıtrat." *Türkiye Diyanet Vakfı Islam Ansiklopedisi* no. 13, 47–48.
Holtzman, Livnat. 2010. "Human Choice, Divine Guidance and the Fitra Tradition: The Use of Hadith in Theological Treatises by Ibn Taymiyya and Ibn Qayyim al-Jawziyya." In *Ibn Taymiyya and His Times*, edited by Yossef Rapoport and Shahab Ahmed, 163–189. Oxford: Oxford University Press.
Hulagü, Mehmet. 2008. *Bir Umudun Insaası: Hicaz Demiryolu*. Izmir: Yitik Hazine Yayinevi.
Ibn Abd Al-Wahhab, Muhammad. 2010. *Kitab al-Tawheed*. Translated by Sameh Strauch. Riyadh, Saudi Arabia: International Islamic Publishing House.
Insoll, Timothy. 1999. *The Archaeology of Islam*. Oxford: Oxford University Press.
Insoll, Timothy. 2007. "Changing Identities in The Arabian Gulf." In *The Archaeology of Identities: A Reader*, edited by Timothy Insoll, 309–321. London: Routledge.
Introduction, The National Museum. 2015 [accessed August 5, 2015]. Available from http://www.nationalmuseum.org.sa/introduction.aspx.
Khan, Majeed. 1993. *Prehistoric Rock Art of Northern Saudi Arabia*. Riyadh, Saudi Arabia: Department of Antiquities and Museums.
Khan, Majeed. 2000. *Wusum: The Tribal Symbols of Saudi Arabia*. Riyadh, Saudi Arabia: Ministry of Education, Deputy Ministry of Antiquities & Museums.
Khan, Majeed. 2007. *Rock Art of Saudi Arabia across Twelve Thousand Years*. Riyadh, Saudi Arabia: Ministry of Education, Deputy Ministry of Antiquities & Museums.
Koloğlu, Orhan. 2017. *Türk-Arap İlişkileri Tarihi*. Istanbul: Tarihçi Kitabevi.

Kuzgun, Saban. 1997. "Hanif." *Türkiye Diyanet Vakfı İslam Ansiklopedisi* no. 16, 33–39.
Leaman, Oliver. 2006. *The Qur'an: An Encyclopedia*. London: Routledge.
Leatherdale, Clive. 1983. *Britain and Saudi Arabia, 1925–1939: The Imperial Oasis*. London: Frank Cass.
Liverani, Mario. 2005. "Imperialism." In *Archaeologies of the Middle East: Critical Perspectives*, edited by Susan Pollock and Reinhard Bernbeck, 223–244. Malden, MA: Blackwell Publishing.
Makdisi, Ussama. 2002. "Ottoman Orientalism." *The American Historical Review* no. 107 (3): 768–796.
Milwright, Marcus. 2009. "Defining Islamic Archaeology—Some Preliminary Notes." *AKPIA@MIT Forum: Studies in Architecture, History, and Culture*:1–11.
Milwright, Marcus. 2010. *An Introduction to Islamic Archaeology*. Edinburgh, UK: Edinburgh University Press.
Nehmé, Laila. 2007. "The Rediscovery of Madâ'in Sâlih, Ancient Hegra, Saudi Arabia." *Bulletin of the Society for Arabian Studies* no. 12, 11–13.
Nicholson, James. 2005. *The Hejaz Railway*. London: Stacey International.
Nizamoglu, Yüksel 2013. "1917 Yilinda Hicaz Cephesi: Arap Isyaninin Yayilmasi ve Medine'nin Tahliyesi Programi." *Biliğ* 66, 123–148.
Noyes, James. 2013. *The Politics of Iconoclasm: Religion, Violence, and the Culture of Image-Breaking in Christianity and Islam*. New York: I.B. Tauris.
Okruhlik, Gwenn. 2004. "Over History and Identity: 'Opening the Gates' of the Kingdom to Tourism." In *Counter-Narratives: History, Contemporary Society, and Politics in Saudi Arabia and Yemen*, edited by Madawi Al-Rasheed and Robert Vitalis, 201–228. New York: Palgrave Macmillan.
Olsen, Sandra L. 2013. *Stories in the Rocks: Exploring Saudi Arabian Rock Art*. Pittsburgh, PA: Carnegie Museum of Natural History.
Orbasli, Aylin, and Simon Woodward 2008. "A Railway 'Route' as a Linear Heritage Attraction: The Hijaz Railway in the Kingdom of Saudi Arabia." *Journal of Heritage Tourism* no. 3 (3): 159–175.
Ozyuksel, Murat. 2014. *The Hejaz Railway: Modernity, Industrialization, and Ottoman Decline*. London: I.B. Tauris.
Petersen, Andrew. 1996. *Dictionary of Islamic Architecture*. New York: Routledge.
Petersen, Andrew. 2014. "Religion in Islamic Archaeology." In *Encyclopedia of Global Archaeology*, edited by Claire Smith, 6268–6276. New York: Springer.
Potts, Daniel T. 1998. "The Gulf Arab States and Their Archaeology." In *Archaeology Under Fire: Nationalism, Politics and Heritage in the Eastern Mediterranean and Middle East*, edited by Lynn Meskell, 189–199. New York: Routledge.

Rice, Michael, and Company Ltd. 1984. Six Site Museums in the Kingdom of Saudi Arabia Part 2, Phase 1: Taima. Riyadh, Saudi Arabia: Department of Antiquities and Museums, Ministry of Education.

Rogan, Eugene L. 1996. "Aşiret Mektebi: Abdulhamid II's School for Tribes (1892–1907)." *International Journal of Middle East Studies* no. 28 (1): 83–107.

Roubille, Auguste. 1900. *Abdul Hamid II, Le Sultan Rouge*. Vol. n°5 Lyon, France: Le Musée de Sires.

Sakaoglu, Necdet. 1999. *Bu Mülkün Sultanlari*. Istanbul: Oglak Yayincilik.

Saunders, Nicholas J., and Neil Faulkner 2010. "Fire on the Desert: Conflict Archaeology and the Great Arab Revolt in Jordan 1916–1918." *Antiquity* no. 84, 514–527.

SCTH. *National Museum, Saudi Commission for Tourism and National Heritage* 2011 [accessed July 31, 2015]. Available from https://www.scta.gov.sa/en/Antiquities-Museums/pages/NationalMuseum.aspx.

SCTH. *Museum Directory, Saudi Commission for Tourism and National Heritage* 2014 [accessed August 2, 2015]. Available from https://www.scta.gov.sa/en/Museums/Pages/MuseumDirectory.aspx.

SCTH. *Our Logo, Saudi Commission for Tourism and National Heritage* 2015 [accessed July 22, 2015]. Available from http://www.scta.gov.sa/en/AboutSCTA/Pages/OurLogo.aspx.

The National Museum. *Pre-Islamic Poems Recited by Young Creative Girls at The National Museum, Saudi Arabia*. The National Museum, Saudi Arabia 2015 [accessed August 1, 2015]. Available from http://www.nationalmuseum.org.sa/LatestNews.aspx?id=229.

UNESCO. *The Hejaz Railway*. UNESCO 2015 [accessed August 1, 2015]. Available from http://whc.unesco.org/en/tentativelists/6026/.

Webb, Peter. 2014. "Al-Jāhiliyya: Uncertain Times of Uncertain Meanings." *Der Islam* no. 91 (1): 69–94.

Yusuf, Ali A. 2000. *The Holy Quran: Translation by Abdullah Yusuf Ali*. Kent, UK: Wordsworth Classics of World Literature.

Zarins, Juris. 1984. "Al-Hofuf, Najran, Jizan, Al-Ula/Taima, Al-Jawf: The Stone Age to the Mid-1st Milleunnium BC." In *Six Site Museums in the Kingdom of Saudi Arabia, Part 3 Research Papers*, edited by Michael Rice and Company Limited, Riyadh: Department of Antiquities and Museums, Ministry of Education.

Ömer Can Aksoy is a PhD candidate at UCL, Qatar, and coordinator of the Battle of Aslıhanlar Project in Turkey. His research interests include ancient warfare in the Arabian Peninsula, wayfinding in archaeological sites, visual communication design, modern conflict archaeology in Turkey, use-wear analysis of metal weaponry, and rock art of Saudi Arabia and Oman.

Open Access This book is licensed under the terms of the Creative Commons Attribution 4.0 International License (http://creativecommons.org/licenses/by/4.0/), which permits use, sharing, adaptation, distribution and reproduction in any medium or format, as long as you give appropriate credit to the original author(s) and the source, provide a link to the Creative Commons license and indicate if changes were made.

The images or other third party material in this chapter are included in the chapter's Creative Commons license, unless indicated otherwise in a credit line to the material. If material is not included in the chapter's Creative Commons license and your intended use is not permitted by statutory regulation or exceeds the permitted use, you will need to obtain permission directly from the copyright holder.

CHAPTER 6

Images of Piety or Power? Conserving the Umayyad Royal Narrative in Qusayr 'Amra

Gaetano Palumbo

Abstract This chapter focuses on the work of conservation at the site of Qusayr 'Amra, a bathhouse located 80 km east of Amman, in Jordan. The site was built by the Umayyad prince Walid b. Yazid during the caliphate of his uncle Hisham, probably between 730 and 743 AD (111–125 H.), and its interior walls are covered by mural paintings. I explore how archaeology and conservation have contributed or interfered with the understanding of the monument, and how authenticity can be defined in a site that has seen at least three major conservation interventions. It will also discuss whether the paintings can really be defined as "Islamic Art," fitting a narrative of royal power that uses symbols and iconographies that are borrowed from the cultures that preceded the arrival of Islam in the region.

Keywords Wall paintings · conservation · Islamic art · Umayyad dynasty · Jordan

G. Palumbo (✉)
UCL Qatar, Doha, Qatar

© The Author(s) 2017
T. Rico (ed.), *The Making of Islamic Heritage*, Heritage Studies in the Muslim World, DOI 10.1007/978-981-10-4071-9_6

Introduction

Numerous studies have been dedicated to the meaning and significance of the mural paintings of Qusayr 'Amra and to their origin and inspiration.[1] Changes in the appearance of the paintings following conservation work conducted for the past five years are providing information that is bound to change our perspective on early Islamic art in a secular environment.[2] This chapter looks at the role that conservation has taken in defining the heritage management of this site, especially in terms of managing questions of authenticity, and how this discipline can either contribute to or interfere with our understanding of the original intentions of the patrons and artists that decorated this monument. I will also debate whether the site's cycle of paintings—although certainly produced under the patronage of an Umayyad prince—can truly be defined as "Islamic art," and how these paintings fit a narrative of royal power developed during the Umayyad and continuing into the Abbasid caliphate. Finally, I will consider the way that contemporary perceptions toward this monument by the local Bedouin community, Jordanian archaeologists and students, and Muslim visitors further complicate the work of conservation of "Islamic heritage," suggesting that we consider the implications of our work for a range of nonexpert attitudes as described in this case study.

Qusayr 'Amra is a magnificent bathhouse built by the Umayyad prince, Walid b. Yazid, during the caliphate of his uncle, Hisham, probably after 730 AD (111 H.) and before becoming caliph himself in 743 AD (125 H.). The building, located in the eastern *badiya* (semi-desert) of Jordan, 80 km east of Amman, is part of a larger complex that includes a *qasr* (palace), a watchtower, complex hydraulic systems, and other unexcavated structures. The paintings contained inside the bathhouse are considered by art historians and archaeologists as an outstanding and unique testimony to early Islamic art, which earned the site its inscription on the United Nations Educational, Scientific, and Cultural Organization's (UNESCO) World Heritage List in 1985.

Qusayr 'Amra is commonly assigned to the broader group of "desert castles," built during Umayyad times in the semi-arid and desert regions of Syria and Jordan. These structures belong to different typologies—caravanserais, palaces, agricultural estates, and, in rare cases, military structures—thus having various purposes, including political and strategic ones. They offered attractive spaces to engage the chiefs of local Bedouin tribes in political discussions while enjoying leisure activities, ensuring that relations with them remained firm while strengthening Umayyad power in the region (**Arce** in press; **Vibert-Guigue and Bisheh** 2007, 13–14). The bathhouse is the main monument building at the site, which displays in its interior a unique cycle of paintings, representing the most extended testimony of figurative art in Umayyad times. They are thus of fundamental importance to disciplinary understandings of the birth and evolution of Islamic art in terms of themes, iconography, and techniques.

The paintings display a rich and articulated iconographic repertoire, where a variety of themes with no apparent unity blend together images, texts, and narratives borrowed from Greek mythology and Sasanian traditions, as well as Byzantine-style portraits, hunting scenes, depictions of animals and birds, court scenes, dances, and even a reference to the Prophet Jonah. The building opens on a main audience hall, parted in three longitudinal aisles, each covered with a vaulted roof and decorated by paintings. The decoration here is divided in two registers: a lower register, from the ground floor to a height of approximately 1.8 meters, and an upper register, up to the top of the walls and also including the vaults. The lower register is characterized by paintings representing marble slabs and *opus sectile*.[3] The upper register hosts a variety of scenes from leisure activities to professional tasks and possibly political engagements. A so-called throne room displays on its south wall a representation of a prince seated under a baldachin. In the main hall, a small opening on the eastern side of the room leads to the bath complex, characterized by a small changing room (*apodyterium*) with a barrel vault, a warm room (*tepidarium*) with a cross vault, and a hot room (*caldarium*) with a dome. All these rooms are decorated with mural paintings in the upper part of the walls and ceilings; the lower parts were originally covered with marble slabs, and, in the *caldarium*, also with wall mosaics, all of which have disappeared.[4] Walls in the main hall feature a number of Arabic Kufic inscriptions: a *basmala* (Imbert as cited in De Palma et al. 2012, 335–336),[5] and a second inscription that was discovered as part of conservation work in 2012, which contains the name of the prince that commissioned the building, Walid b. Yazid, who became caliph in 743.[6] Cleaning work also revealed images, including a completely naked swimming naiad and a boat with fishermen pulling up a net full of fish (Vibert-Guigue and Bisheh 2007, Pl. 31). This is not the only example of naked or bare-chested female figures, and these are not exclusively found in Qusayr 'Amra, as they are also present in decorative stuccoes in Qasr al-Hayr al-Gharbi and Khirbet el-Mafjar (Fowden 2004a, 72–73). Despite these potentially contradicting features, the inscription of this site in the World Heritage List in 1985 recognized the uniqueness of the paintings and their role in the formation of "Islamic art."

Conservation at Qusayr 'Amra: Revealing the Authentic?

The uniqueness of Qusayr 'Amra as a conservation site lies in the relatively good state of preservation of its mural paintings. This may be due to a series of factors: the remoteness of the area where the site is located, the use of the building as a shelter by the Bedouin tribes of the region, and the layers of soot generated by campfires lit in its interior that contributed to protecting the paintings from deterioration or vandalism. Moreover, some graffiti left on the walls by pilgrims and travelers between the fourteenth and sixteenth centuries seem to indicate a certain respect for the site and the mysterious representations that must have fascinated the travelers who stopped there on their way to Mecca. The first substantial conservation effort was conducted between 1974 and 1975, by a team from the Madrid Archaeological Museum. The cleaning of the site revealed many more details than what Musil and the painter Mielich had recorded in their short survey of the site in 1901, when they also used some hard chemicals in order to see the paintings below the soot layers, resulting in some damage. Moreover, in order to enhance the figures, the Spanish conservators decided to outline their profiles with new paint, in some cases adding details, without documenting or announcing this intervention. This work (Almagro Basch et al. 1975), a French-Jordanian project conducted between 1989 and 1995 (Vibert-Guigue and Bisheh 2007), and the most recent conservation project that started in 2010 that has taken advantage of advances in conservation methods and tools, have together transformed—in some cases quite radically—our understanding and interpretation of the figures represented on the walls of the monument (De Palma et al. 2012; De Palma 2013).

Four Arabic inscriptions have so far been identified in Qusayr 'Amra, and they provide us with a clear indication of the owner of the building: Walid b. Yazid. However, only the one recently rediscovered on top of the western aisle's south wall mentions him explicitly by name. The inscription found on the baldachin of the throne (in the so-called throne room) is a simple invocation mentioning the prince as the heir apparent (Imbert 2007). The third inscription, on top of the south wall of the eastern aisle of the main hall, references David and Abraham. The fourth inscription, located below a scene representing the prince and his attendants on the south wall of the western aisle, is the largest and framed in a *tabula ansata*.[7] Conservation work confirmed this to be a *basmala*, written in very large characters. With the

Fig. 6.1 Two of the "kings" before and after conservation. The 1975 intervention did not allow the perception of the "real" quality of the paintings (Photographs by Gaetano Palumbo, 2012)

exception of the *basmala*, all other inscriptions begin with *Allahumma* (O Allah), each asking God to provide blessing, forgiveness, or virtue to the prince. The one asking for virtue is associated with the representation of the Prophet Jonah just below it, and on the same wall we have the prince attended by a scribe, a servant, and two children who are perhaps his sons. Conservation of this scene revealed the character in the center of the composition to be a portrait of al-Walid, himself, and not a woman, as almost all scholars had previously supposed (De Palma et al. 2012, 175ff.; Fowden 2004a).

The field of conservation tackles this site in terms of the challenge of managing issues of authenticity, as each modern intervention left a trace on top of the original layers. Conservation principles consider that newer interventions can rightly claim to have revealed paintings closest to the original, but modern interventions have also modified the conditions of the building and its paintings. While the 1975 "enhancements" caused wrong attribution and interpretation—even causing several scholars to declare that the paintings were not of great quality (Vibert-Guigue and Bisheh 2007, 7)—the latest conservation work is now calling into question the interpretation and understanding of the areas of the monument that remain to be cleaned, reevaluating the artists' technical skills and the background that brought them to create this masterpiece (Fig. 6.1).

Is the Art of Qusayr ʿAmra "Islamic"?

The complexity of the iconography found in Qusayr ʿAmra has provided grounds for debate among art historians and archaeologists since the site was published by Musil in the early twentieth century, and contributes to the debate on what it means to speak of "Islamic art." While Grabar (1973, 2) has argued that "Islamic art" does not define religion, but rather, a cultural movement that modifies and spreads over local traditions, Wijdan Ali (1999) considers that the appropriation of motifs and symbols derived from other cultures and the term "Islamic" are not in contradiction. According to Ali (1999, 13), Islamic art

> can include any artistic manifestation created by a Muslim or non-Muslim artist that adheres to Islamic aesthetics, principles and concepts, and that is created for the spiritual, intellectual, and physical usage and enjoyment of Muslims or non-Muslims living within the sphere of Islamic thought and civilization.

This broader definition of "Islamic art" includes, especially for the early centuries of Islam, all the artistic traditions with which Muslims entered into contact and from which they chose, according to Ali, whatever suited their taste and beliefs. On the issue of figurative representations, Ali (1999, 14–15) insists on the fact that the two sayings attributed to Mohammed forbidding figurative representations were intended to discourage idolatry in places of worship, and did not mean a total ban of this artistic form, referring in particular to the miniature artistic tradition of Iran, Afghanistan, India, and Ottoman Turkey. In addition, in their extensive essay fittingly entitled "The Mirage of Islamic Art," Blair and Bloom (2003, 152) consider that most Islamic art was not made for the purposes of the faith, citing a lack of evidence to support the claim that artists and patrons would have called the art they produced "Islamic." They consequently argue that the notion of an "Islamic" tradition in the arts and architecture in places where Islam was the main religion is a Western construct—a product of late nineteenth- and early-twentieth-century scholarship (Blair and Bloom 2003, 153). Within a Western perspective, then, the art of Qusayr 'Amra is Islamic, given that it is the product of artists who clearly worked under the patronage of an Umayyad prince, and who used iconographic motifs that were readily available in the common repertoire of late antique art—especially Byzantine and Sasanian—to celebrate the power of the Umayyads. However, if the term "Islamic" is used to indicate not religion, but rather, the influence that Islam has on all aspects of life in the Muslim world, then it becomes more difficult to justify the presence and categorization of so many non-Islamic elements in the wall paintings of this monument. In this perspective, the art of Qusayr 'Amra may not be "Islamic" after all but may rather represent a phenomenon of acculturation or cultural appropriation by the Umayyads, used to reinforce their claims over newly conquered lands through the deployment of symbols and iconographies that were still well known and remembered from previous narratives of power.

An example of this process is the presence of Jonah that was revealed by conservation work at different locations among the mural paintings of Qusayr ʿAmra (Fig. 6.2). This intriguing feature raises the question of whether this composition makes reference to the virtue that the prince would like God to help him achieve.

Before conservation work clearly revealed this feature on the south and north walls of the western aisle, only a small scene under the throne of the prince on the back wall of the throne room was visible, representing Jonah being thrown into the sea with a marine monster approaching.[8] Jonah's story is found both in the Bible and in the Qur'an, and the presence of the prophet in proximity to the prince not once, but twice, certainly carries symbolic value.[9] Fontana (2012) sees this as a demonstration of the fact that early Islam needed "to relate its origin to a universal past, replacing

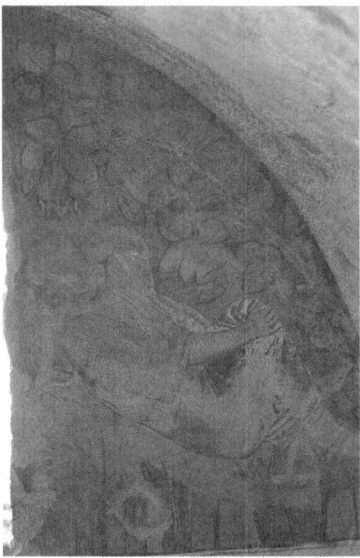

Fig. 6.2 One of the numerous representations of Prophet Jonah found in Qusayr ʿAmra (Photograph by Gaetano Palumbo, 2012)

Judaism and Christianity, but as a new sponsor of God's legacy and speaking the same language." What remains unclear, however, is why the artists decided to paint these episodes in three different locations in the building rather than in a logical sequence.

Imbert (in press) argues that the inscriptions at Qusayr ʿAmra should not be seen in association with the paintings; rather, he argues that together with the paintings, they provide an intimate portrait of al-Walid and give a glimpse of his aspirations to power. Fowden (2004a), on the other hand, looks at Qusayr ʿAmra's paintings through the lens of Arab ode poetry (*qasida*), arguing that

> all [paintings] were...loosely linked together by the architectural framework that contained them, and by a general theme of princely panegyric or at least celebration of princely life. The resemblance to the qa[si]da extended, in other words, beyond the shared themes of love, hunting, and panegyric...to embrace also a fundamental structural affinity.

This is illustrated in the *qasida* "panel" structure, which is also how the paintings in Qusayr ʿAmra can be described. However, Fowden (2004a, 315) concludes that the paintings at the site "attest a rather advanced stage of Mediterranean inculturation (sic) on the part of the Umayyad patron and his immediate circle."

Alami (2011, 69) is convinced instead that there is a strict and unequivocal relationship between early Islamic architecture and the principles of Arabic theory of language and poetics. The symbolic association between *qasida* (praise hymns) and *madih* (panegyrics), palatial architecture and use of space, and continuous references to Bacchic culture (including wine poetry and sexual references) are arguments used by Ali (2008) to support the idea that Abbasid caliphs adopted a henotheistic position to enforce their power through the definition of sacred kingship and the acceptance of ancient Near Eastern models of authority. In this perspective, we must look at numerous Dionysian references (e.g., vines, grapes, panthers, music, dances) in the paintings of Qusayr ʿAmra,[10] and I would argue that they should be seen not as a sign of al-Walid's eccentricity or interest in the Classical world but rather as part of a symbolic repertoire of themes and motifs that support the image of the caliph's power (Fig. 6.3).

Against the doctrine that took shape in the early centuries of Sunni Islam, in which the caliph should be an elected steward of the Muslim community

IMAGES OF PIETY OR POWER? CONSERVING THE UMAYYAD ROYAL... 99

Fig. 6.3 Standing figure holding a basket of grapes, flanked by a feline (a panther?)—perhaps a representation of Dionysus (Photograph by Gaetano Palumbo, 2014)

and successor of the Prophet, the Umayyad and Abbasid dynasties used the title *Khalifat Allah* (successor to God) to imply a notion of kingship (Al-Azmeh 2001, 74–77; Crone and Hinds 2012, 11–16). Marsham (2009) thinks that the references to Adam, Abraham, and David—all found on the south-facing walls and thereby facing Mecca—are particularly relevant for al-Walid's claim of a covenant between the Umayyad dynasty and God himself. In early Qur'anic exegesis, Adam is humanity's representative in taking the first covenant with God, Abraham is the founder of Islam, and while David is the king chosen by God.

The painting of the "six kings" on the western wall of the main hall of Qusayr 'Amra (Vibert-Guigue and Bisheh 2007, Pl. 28),[11] together with the image of the enthroned prince on the southern wall of the "throne room" (Vibert-Guigue and Bisheh 2007, Pl. 15), is perhaps the clearest political statement used by al-Walid (Fig. 6.4).[12]

Fig. 6.4 The so-called Six Kings panel, either representing the kings defeated by the Umayyads, the six regions of the Earth, or the recipients of Prophet Mohammad's embassies (Photograph by Gaetano Palumbo, 2013)

The kings are clearly represented with their hands turned towards their right, in the act of paying respect. The recent discovery that the main figure represented in the scene to the right of the kings is male (and not female, as previously thought) confirms the idea that the kings are indeed honoring the prince, as maintained by some scholars (Fowden 2004a; Grabar 1954, 1980). Earlier interpretations (Creswell 1932) saw in this scene a representation of the kings defeated by the Umayyads, based on Musil's (1907) interpretation of the second king from the left as Roderic, the Visigoth king of Hispania defeated by the Umayyads in the battle of

Guadalete in 712 AD (93 H.). Grabar's (1954) view is that this scene finds its roots in the Sasanian tradition of the "Kings of the Earth," with the Umayyads claiming to be "the descendant and heir of the dynasties it had defeated." Fowden (2004a, 197–226, 2004b) wrote extensively on the topic, reaching the conclusion that this representation of "six kings" (plus a seventh, the prince, or rather the Umayyad dynasty) finds its inspiration in the Sasanian conception of the Empire in the center of the earth surrounded by six geopolitical regions (India and Sub-Saharan Africa, Arabia, North Africa and Spain, Rum, Turkic Central Asia, and China), which in his opinion correspond to the kings represented in the painting. This Sasanian worldview would have then been appropriated by the Umayyads for their own definition of kingship. Di Branco (2007) thinks instead that this scene is a reference to the sending of embassies by Mohammed to the "six kings of the Earth" in the year 6 H (628 AD), and in particular to the Byzantine Caesar, the Sasanian Chosroe, the Abyssinian Negus, the Egyptian Muqawqis (the Coptic patriarch), the Ghassanid philarch (al-Harit b. Abi Simr), and the lord of Yamamah (Hawdah b. Ali al-Hanafi). If Di Branco's hypothesis is correct, why should they be paying homage to al-Walid? Did the artists perhaps intend to have the kings pointing to the large *basmala* inscription, which is also located just to the left of the kings' figures? In this case, the kings would be represented as recognizing the truth of Allah's word and the authority of Mohammed as his representative. This interpretation may not be so far-fetched: Although Walid b. Yazid did not enjoy a good reputation,[13] recent interpretation credits him with theologically significant innovations, especially with respect the role of the caliph as Allah's representative. According to Judd (2008),

> [Walid b. Yazid] cannot be dismissed as a drunken playboy or a reckless failure as caliph. Instead, despite his obvious faults, he was theologically literate and formulated doctrinal foundations for even his most egregious actions. While he may have been the Umayyad family's most pernicious sinner, he may also have been their most competent religious thinker.

As Qusayr 'Amra's patron, Walid b. Yazid undoubtedly left a clear mark on the paintings. However, contrary to some interpretations, they are not the illustration of his hedonism or are they there to fulfill one person's "dream." Rather, they perfectly fit the Umayyad narrative of power, drawing elements from Hellenistic, Roman, Byzantine, and Sasanian repertoires and ideals that best described the Umayyad worldview, and especially its notion of kingship.[14] These elements were re-elaborated into a new visual paradigm, which resulted in Qusayr 'Amra as the most complete expression of the Umayyad concept of *Khalifat Allah*.

What Can Qusayr 'Amra Do for "Islamic Heritage"?

Beyond an art historical interpretation of the site that is carried out in conjunction with conservation interventions, the recent development of a site management plan at Qusayr 'Amra further complicates the issue of how to interpret the site's imagery. This management plan was conducted in consultation with the local community, the Bani Sakhr Bedouin tribe. As part of the planning process, seminars and activities were also organized for students from the Faculty of Heritage and Tourism at the Hashemite University in Zarqa, including the use of formal interviews with tourists visiting the site. An interesting split was noticed between these different demographics. The local community had an understanding of the antiquity of the site and of its origin as a place belonging to a Muslim prince, but for them the value of the place was associated with the natural environment, which includes a *wadi* (valley) rich in water during winter and spring, and a growth of ancient terebinth trees, where one could find excellent pasture and hunting grounds (it is important to note in this regard that the themes of hunting and water are a constant presence in the paintings of Qusayr 'Amra). The monument in their perception is an accessory that is conducive to the persistence of their traditional mode of life and production in a particular environment. This engagement with stakeholders strongly suggests that, despite changes in the interpretation of the "Islamic art" of Qusayr 'Amra, the site does not have an "Islamic" value for some groups. The local intellectual community, instead, feels strongly that the monument is part of an "Islamic" heritage, although not in a religious, but rather in a political sense. Archaeologists and art historians, in contrast, are excited about the new discoveries derived from the conservation activities, as they provide new data on the evolution of artistic techniques and figurative motifs in the first centuries of Islamic power in the region (pers. comm.).

Most Muslim visitors did not seem to have problems with the representations found on the walls of Qusayr 'Amra, as they seemed willing to trace a distinction between public and private spaces, although some of them were perplexed at the presence of a *basmala* under the image of the prince and his attendants. But also in this case they were seeing this as a historic site, with little bearing on religious matters or Islam. The students that assisted in the project and their professors were from different regions of Jordan, not from the local Bedouin community. Several of them expressed strong opposition to defining this monument "Islamic." Some, following a more rigid interpretation of the Qur'an, thought that the figurative representations depicted on the monument could not qualify as "Islamic art," and while the monument may have belonged to Walid b. Yazid (who is still seen in a very negative light by many Muslims), they were convinced that it must have been decorated by Christian artists. Others, however, held a more liberal attitude, in line with the approach of the majority of archaeologists, and did not have any issue with considering the art "Islamic," and the monument an excellent example of a heritage ("their" heritage) reaching far back to the origins of Islam in the region.

Attitudes and perceptions toward this monument among the Jordanian and, in general, Muslim communities, display an entire spectrum of opinions and preconceptions, ranging from a definite attribution to the sphere of "Islamic art" (with the additional value of being one of the monuments where the formation of "Islamic art" can be studied), to a variegated acceptance of it also as "Islamic heritage," to a total rejection of it being Islamic on the basis of what are perceived as blasphemous contents. These examples show that, especially for the formative period of Islam, contemporary Muslim societies are split on the value systems that should be adopted to understand and explain apparent contradictions in the way early Muslim societies approached the matter of artistic representation. This is also partly due to Western scholarship, which has imposed categories that may not properly reflect the relationships between the private and the public sphere in Muslim societies across time. A disjunction between the public and the intellectual elite is also at play here, as the latter has not been able to inform and interest the public in the depth and complexity of Islamic heritage beyond simplistic and reductive understandings. In the case of Qusayr 'Amra specifically, and with respect to the figurative arts produced in an Islamic context more generally, it is perhaps useful to speak of "Islamic heritage(s)," in order to maintain, on one hand, the idea that Islam does permeate all aspects of life, including artistic expressions, and on the other hand, to admit that within Islam there are groups that look at heritage through lenses that are not exclusively focused on Islamic principles and dogmas.

Notes

1. See especially Almargo Basch et al., *Qusayr 'Amra: Residencia y baños en el desierto de Jordania*; Blázquez Martínez, *Las Pinturas Helenísticas de Qusayr 'Amra (Jordania) y sus Fuentes*; Creswell, *Early Muslim Architecture*; Fowden, *Qusayr 'Amra: Art and the Umayyad Elite in Late Antique Syria*; Fowden and Fowden, *Studies in Hellenism, Christianity and the Ummayads*; Grabar, *The Paintings at Qusayr Amrah: The Private Art of an Umayyad Prince*; Musil, *Kuseir 'Amra*; and Vibert-Guigue and Bisheh, *Qusayr 'Amra: Un Bain Omeyyade dans la Bâdiya Jordanienne*.
2. Conservation work at Qusayr 'Amra has being conducted since 2010, by a team of Italian conservators from the *Istituto Superiore per la Conservazione ed il Restauro* (ISCR—Higher Institute for Conservation and Restoration) in partnership with the World Monuments Fund (WMF) and the Department of Antiquities of Jordan.
3. *Opus sectile* refers to an ancient and medieval art technique in which cut stones of various types and shapes are set in walls and floors in order to make pictures or patterns.
4. For a comprehensive documentation and description of this monument, see the work published by Vibert Guigue and Bisheh (2007). High-resolution photographs of all the paintings were taken by the recent conservation mission and will be made available to the public in the near future on the websites of the ISCR at: http://www.icr.beniculturali.it and the WMF at: https://www.wmf.org/project/qusayr-amra.
5. A *Basmala* is the name of the Islamic phrase "*b-ismi-llāhi r-raḥmāni r-raḥīm*," meaning "In the name of God, the Most Gracious, the Most Merciful."
6. The inscription cannot be read in its entirety, but in fragments only. The first of its three lines, however, does not leave any doubts as to the name of Walid b. Yazid. Imbert (as cited in De Palma et al. 2012, 332–333) proposes a first reading as being, "O God, make al-Walid bin Yazid virtuous the way you did with your pious servants! Surround him with the freshness of mercy, O Lord of the Worlds, and for your community, eternal... the religion the day of... all the... " A second reading is proposed in a new article (Imbert 2016, 332), where the second and third lines are given a slightly different meaning. The first line containing the name of the prince is confirmed in the second reading. As the inscription does not contain any reference to al-Walid already being caliph, we can date the building to the years when he was the heir apparent under the reign of his uncle, Hisham. Two C-14 dates, obtained from charcoal found in the *caldarium* and *tepidarium* of the bath, date the building and its use to the year 730 AD ± 20, thus confirming the epigraphic evidence (De Palma 2013, 427).

7. A *tabula ansata* is a tablet with dovetail handles, and in Roman and Byzantine contexts contained votive or dedicatory inscriptions; it is not rare in Islamic contexts as well (Blair 1992, 18–19; Fowden 2004a, 178; Sharon 1999, 54).
8. Most of this scene was detached by Musil in 1902 and is now at the Pergamon Museum in Berlin.
9. On the left, the Prophet Jonah is represented above the figure of the prince, in a pensive pose, while on the right he is represented as sleeping under a tree—a reference to an episode narrated in the Bible in which he falls asleep after having failed to convert the people of Nineveh, and God makes a gourd tree grow so as to provide him with shade (Book of Jonah, Chapter 4, verses 5–6). In the Qur'an (Sura 37, as-Saffat, 146), Allah makes the gourd tree grow "above him" on the beach where the marine monster casts him out (De Palma et al. 2012, 330–331, figs. 22–24). On the opposite wall, Jonah is represented as being swallowed by a marine monster and subsequently cast on the beach (Book of Jonah, chapter 4; Qur'an, Sura 37, as-Saffat, verses 142–145.)
10. See, for example, the recently discovered painting of a panther besides the lower part of a standing figure holding a basket full of grapes on the vault of the western aisle (Figure 6.3), or the representation of Dionysus discovering Ariadne sleeping on a beach in Naxos, on the western lunette of the *apodyterium* (Vibert-Guigue and Bisheh 2007, Pl. 64, left).
11. Inscriptions above the heads of the kings qualify at least three of them as kings or emperors: the Byzantine Caesar, the Sasanian Chosroe, and the Negus of Abissinia.
12. This representation finds interesting parallels in Byzantine iconography, such as Adam sitting on a throne in a Syrian mosaic (Fowden 2004a, 136), and in innumerable early Christian representations of Christ *Pantocrator* (i.e., "Ruler of All Things").
13. Judd (2008) describes how Walid b. Yazid was vilified in Abbasid propaganda and taken as an example of Umayyad excesses.
14. According to Canepa (2009, 224), "The private appropriation of Roman and Sasanian cosmocratic ideals by the Umayyad elite provided the raw material for their eclectic imaginings of power, initiating a process of reinvention and reinvigoration that coalesced on a more public stage with the Abbasids and their successor states."

Bibliography

Alami, Mohammed Hamdouni. 2011. *Art and Architecture in the Islamic Tradition: Aesthetics, Politics and Desire in Early Islam*. London: I.B. Tauris.

Al-Azmeh, Aziz. 2001. *Muslim Kingship. Power and the Sacred in Muslim, Christian and Pagan Polities*. London: I.B. Tauris.
Ali, Samer M. 2008. "Early Islam—Monotheism or Henotheism? A View from the Court." *Journal of Arabic Literature* no. 39: 14–37.
Ali, Wijdan. 1999. *The Arab Contribution to Islamic Art from the Seventh to the Fifteenth Centuries*. Cairo and Amman: The American University in Cairo Press and the Royal Society for Fine Arts, Jordan.
Almagro Basch, Martín, Luis Caballero, Juan Zoreda, Zozaya Stabel-Hansen, and Antonio Almagro. 1975. *Qusayr 'Amra,: Residencia y baños en el desierto de Jordania*. Madrid: Instituto Hispano-Árabe de Cultura.
Arce, Ignacio. in press. "Dionysus in the Hamman: Notes on the Survival of Hellenistic Pagan Culture in Late Antiquity and Early Islam." In *The Colors of the Prince: Proceedings of the 2014 International Conference on Qusayr 'Amra*, edited by De Palma, Giovanna. Rome: Istituto Superiore per la Conservazione e il Restauro.
Blair, Sheila S. 1992. *The Monumental Inscriptions from Early Islamic Iran and Transoxiana*. Leiden, Netherlands: Brill.
Blair, Sheila S., and Jonathan M. Bloom. 2003. "The Mirage of Islamic Art: Reflections on the Study of an Unwieldy Field." *The Art Bulletin* no. 85 (1): 152–184.
Canepa, Matthew P. 2009. *The Two Eyes of the Earth: Art and Ritual of Kingship between Rome and Sasanian Iran*. Berkeley: University of California Press.
Creswell, Keppel Archibald Cameron. 1932. *Early Muslim Architecture*. Vol. 1. Oxford: Clarendon Press.
Crone, Patricia, and Martin Hinds. 2012. *God's Caliph: Religious Authority in the First Centuries of Islam*. Cambridge: Cambridge University Press.
De Palma, Giovanna. 2013. "Qusayr 'Amra World Heritage Site: Preliminary Report on Documentation, Conservation and Site Management Activities in 2012–2013." *Annual of the Department of Antiquities of Jordan* no. 57: 425–439.
De Palma, Giovanna, Gaetano Palumbo, Carlo Birrozzi, Marie-José Mano, Maria Carolina Gaetani, Asma Shhaltoug, Mohammed Al-Khatib, and Frédéric Imbert. 2012. "Qusayr 'Amra World Heritage Site: Preliminary Report on Documentation, Conservation and Site Management Activities in 2010–2012." *Annual of the Department of Antiquities of Jordan* no. 56: 309–340.
Di Branco, Marco. 2007. "I Sei Principi di Qusayr 'Amrah fra Tardoantico, Ellenismo e Islam." *Rendiconti dell'Accademia Nazionale dei Lincei* no. 18 (4): 597–620.
Fontana, Maria Vittoria. 2012. "Su una Possibile Raffigurazione della Storia di Giona a Qusayr 'Amra." *Rivista degli Studi Orientali* no. 85 (1–4): 279–303.
Fowden, Garth. 2004a. *Qusayr 'Amra: Art and the Umayyad Elite in Late Antique Syria*. Berkeley: University of California Press.

Fowden, Garth. 2004b. "The Six Kings at Qusayr 'Amra." In *La Persia e Bisanzio: Convegno Internazionale (Roma, 14–18 Ottobre 2002)*, edited by Antonio Carile, 263–273. Rome: Accademia Nazionale dei Lincei.

Fowden, Garth, and Elizabeth Key Fowden 2004. *Studies in Hellenism, Christianity and the Umayyads, Mélétèmata, 37.* Athens: Research Center for Greek and Roman Antiquity.

Grabar, Oleg. 1954. "The Painting of the Six Kings at Qusayr 'Amrah." *Ars Orientalis* no. 1: 185–187.

Grabar, Oleg. 1973. *The Formation of Islamic Art.* New Haven, CT: Yale University Press.

Grabar, Oleg. 1980. *The Paintings at Qusayr Amrah: The Private Art of an Umayyad Prince.* Los Angeles: Getty Research Institute.

Imbert, Frédéric. 2007. "Inscription Peinte sur le Baldaquin des Bains de Qusayr 'Amra: Note Épigraphique et Paléographique." In *Qusayr 'Amra: Un Bain Omeyyade dans la Bâdiya Jordanienne*, edited by Claude Vibert-Guigue, Ghazi Bisheh, and Frédéric Imbert, 45–46. Beirut: Institute Français du Proche-Orient.

Imbert, Frédéric. 2016. "Le Prince al-Walid et son Bain: Itinéraires Épigraphiques à Qusayr 'Amra." *Bulletin d'Études Orientales* no. 64: 321–363.

Judd, Steven. 2008. "Reinterpreting al-Walīd b. Yazīd." *Journal of the American Oriental Society* no. 128 (3): 439–458.

Marsham, Andrew. 2009. *Rituals of Islamic Monarchy: Accession and Succession in the First Muslim Empire.* Edinburgh: Edinburgh University Press.

Martínez, Blázquez, and María. José. 1981. "Las Pinturas Helenísticas de Qusayr 'Amra (Jordania) y sus Fuentes." *Archivo Español de Arqueología* no. 54 (143–144): 157–202.

Musil, Alois. 1907. *Kuseir 'Amra.* Vol. 1 and 2. Vienna, Austria: Kaiserliche Akademie der Wissenschaften.

Sharon, Moshe. 1999. *Corpus Inscriptionum Arabicarum Palaestinae.* Vol. 2. Leiden, Netherlands: Brill.

Vibert-Guigue, Claude, and Ghazi Bisheh. 2007. *Qusayr 'Amra: Un Bain Omeyyade dans la Bâdiya Jordanienne.* Beirut: Institute Français du Proche-Orient.

Gaetano Palumbo is researcher at UCL Qatar, in Doha, Qatar. He collaborates with various organizations, including World Monuments Fund, ICCROM, ICOMOS, UNESCO, and the Abu Dhabi Tourism and Culture Authority on projects concerning the conservation, documentation, and management of archaeological sites.

Open Access This book is licensed under the terms of the Creative Commons Attribution 4.0 International License (http://creativecommons.org/licenses/by/4.0/), which permits use, sharing, adaptation, distribution and reproduction in any medium or format, as long as you give appropriate credit to the original author(s) and the source, provide a link to the Creative Commons license and indicate if changes were made.

The images or other third party material in this chapter are included in the chapter's Creative Commons license, unless indicated otherwise in a credit line to the material. If material is not included in the chapter's Creative Commons license and your intended use is not permitted by statutory regulation or exceeds the permitted use, you will need to obtain permission directly from the copyright holder.

CHAPTER 7

The Buddha Remains: Heritage Transactions in Taxila, Pakistan

Hassan Asif and Trinidad Rico

Abstract This chapter offers a perspective from ethnographic heritage research on the preservation of Buddhist artifacts in the Muslim community of Taxila, Pakistan. While this form of heritage preservation practice and art may be interpreted as paradoxical, we discuss social, institutional, and political factors that are responsible for the revival and continuation of these heritage practices. Through the examination of this case study, we discuss a unique mode of engaging with the negotiation of past and present spiritual identities that resists the assumption that this is a territory of heritage in conflict.

Keywords Pre-Islamic · vernacularization · art · ethnographic heritage · Pakistan

SEARCHING FOR THE BUDDHAS

The traveler going from Islamabad toward Taxila can notice that the road is marked by numerous workshops and display centers showcasing items such as stone vases, lamps, tiles, and other decorative objects: Taxila is

---

H. Asif (✉)
UNESCO Pakistan, Islamabad, Pakistan

T. Rico
Rutgers University, New Brunswick, New Jersey, USA

famous in Pakistan for its traditional stone craft industry. These objects are decorated using geometric or floral patterns with little or no use of anthropomorphic or zoomorphic iconographic elements, something that may be expected in this Muslim region. However, what is not seen in these displays are the Buddhist statues that the very same stone-sculptors of Taxila are also creating. This relatively hidden practice is well known in local circles and owes its continuing existence to Taxila's history as an important Buddhist center. As a secret practice, to find an artisan who is willing to display the "Buddhist side" of his craft is a challenging task.

Earning the trust and gaining access to the experience of artisans who engage in the making of Buddhist statues in this unlikely contemporary context is a process that suggests this may be a case study in dissonant heritage and the challenges involved in its preservation. However, as this chapter argues, the experience and modes of engagement of these Muslim artisans with the creation of non-Muslim heritage objects suggests a more nuanced subaltern construction of these heritage practices that is created in association with and through mediation of specific social milieus and opportunities.

This discussion begins just off the main road to the Taxila Museum, where a street spirals through the village of Khan Babar and leads to an abandoned train station. From there, Raheem took convoluting turns into other smaller alleys to finally stop in front of a house with a small gate.[1] He passed through the gate and entered a courtyard in which there were a few chairs, a coffee table, and a pedestal fan. There was nothing out of the ordinary in this courtyard except for a number of miniature yet conspicuous Buddha statuettes standing on a small table by the fan. Over the course of this first meeting, Raheem unveiled Buddha statues of all sizes from behind plant pots in the courtyard, from inside cabinets, and from storage boxes (Fig. 7.1). Raheem is a practicing Muslim who makes stone sculptures of the Buddha for a living. Although he is a master sculptor, he does not openly display or talk about his skills. Like most sculptors in Taxila, Raheem inherited the craft from his forefathers. In the early twentieth century, Raheem's grandfather worked as a contractual laborer for British archaeologists in Taxila. That is when his grandfather was first exposed to the Gandharan Buddhist sculptures. Being a stonemason, he soon realized the economic potential of this craft when he witnessed the extent to which British archeologists valued the excavated sculptures. In his time off, he practiced making sculptures with Gandharan characteristics using the local green schist stone. Raheem asserted that this is when the

Fig. 7.1 Buddhist relic caskets placed in front of Islamic calligraphy with "Allah" inscribed on the stone (left); schist stone lying by the gate of Raheem's house (center); Buddha sculpture in the *bodhisattva* stage, unveiled from behind a plant pot (right) (Photographs by Hassan Asif, 2014)

Gandharan Buddhist sculpture was revived in Taxila after hundreds of years. Raheem's father then learnt the craft after witnessing the high price paid for his own father's works. He quit his job to focus solely on making these replicas.

Taxila is and was during this period a predominantly Muslim community in a predominantly Muslim state. There is, therefore, an expectation of conflict in reference to how Muslim Taxila perceives the construction and circulation of sculptures of the Buddha, and by association, about the artisans who have to negotiate their craft between their private spaces and their public life. To fully appreciate these tensions requires an understanding of the place of Islam in this specific context and how it is associated with particular preconceptions with regards to artistic values in the realm of the arts in Pakistan. On the one hand, the parameters of what constitutes authorized art have been dominated by discussions of the relative tolerance of idolatry (De Glopper 2014 on intermediary traders and antique runners;

Elias 2012; Noyes 2013). A relevant reflection in this discussion is the fate of the Bamiyan Buddhas in 2001, destroyed by the Afghan Taliban in accordance with ultraconservative Salafist precepts (Hussain 2015). Less well publicized is the similar case of the Jahanabad Buddha located in Swat, Pakistan (Rose 2007)—believed to be the largest rock carving of the Buddha in the world (Khaliq 2016)—whose face was dynamited by the Pakistani Taliban in 2007. These are the issues that immediately spring to mind when we consider the construction and stewardship of Buddha statues by Muslims in contemporary times. On the other hand, local response in Pakistan toward this type of reaction to Buddhist imagery has been polarized. Officially, the Pakistani government condemned the attack, with then President Pervez Musharraf sending Lieutenant Moinuddin Haider to prevent the destruction through persuasion (Zaeef 2011). The public reaction was varied: some supported the Taliban's action and rationale of erasing "false idols" from the land, along with ratifying Mullah Omer's statement that "all we are breaking are stones" (Stone and Farchakh Bajjaly 2008, 93); others, especially the literati, mourned the collective loss suffered by humankind (Hussain 2015).

This chapter considers how the creation of Buddha statues in this specific Muslim contemporary context can be understood to reflect two worldviews: a dominant heritage approach focusing on identifying and managing any conflict of values, and an ethnographic approach that reveals individual negotiations of public and private lives on the part of the artisans themselves. Therefore, this discussion will highlight the existence of Buddha statues in Taxila as a reality that reflects the operation of two ontologies: first, a negotiation of values that juxtapose debates in Islam about representational art and heritage practices that attempt to mediate different sets of coexisting values, and second, the practices and attitudes to the construction of Buddhist art from the perspective of artists like Raheem. The latter emphasizes the significance and contribution of ethnographic approaches to the study of heritage value, in particular as a strategy for avoiding essentialized and decontextualized appraisals of any iteration of Islamic values in situ.

Representational Art in Heritage Practices of Taxila

It has been extensively argued that heritage values always operate on multiple conflicting planes, which despite potentially insurmountable differences, can and should be managed to reach consensus and enable preservation (Kang 2009; Nagaoka 2011; Van Der Valk 2014). Though the challenges faced by such an approach have been oversimplified, it nevertheless remains central to how events, such as the Taliban's destruction of the Bamiyan Buddhas, are discussed in heritage debates. A notable feature of this type of analysis is the legitimization and hierarchization of certain forms of heritage value ascribed by particular institutions over other values. In this sense, forms of expertise that engage in this work of mediation are in a position to potentially create a conflict between values that may otherwise be stratified and amalgamated in more productive ways. This chapter suggest, therefore, that we need to consider a correlation between the production of conflicting heritage values and the practice of expert and institutional heritage preservation, where one ontology has to give way for the other one to be realized. As it has been argued that heritage preservation as a practice is in itself destructive of other forms of engagement with material culture (Karlström 2005; Layton et al. 2001), we consider that heritage concerns as an ontology may be incompatible with understanding ways in which artisans like Raheem negotiate their own lifeworlds. In addition, the creation of Buddha statues is entangled with a vernacular heritage discourse in which economic, institutional, and ideological subjectivities are intertwined.

However, because of the dominant concern with destruction in heritage preservation as a field (Rico 2016), entanglements of Buddhist heritage value in Muslim contexts have been mostly articulated in terms of concerns with iconoclasm. The destruction of the Bamiyan Buddhas has been used as a defining case study in heritage to characterize the problem of attitudes to idolatry in Islamic contexts and has included concerns with international law (Francioni and Lenzerini 2003; Mani 2001) and with the localized construction of such art in the Bamiyan valley (Dupree 2002; Levi 1972; Reza 2012). When detached from these dominant heritage debates, the relationship between Buddhist representational art and Islamic contexts takes a different tone. This relationship has shifted significantly in accordance to changing attitudes through time (Elias 2012), variations from individual to individual (Flood 2002), and changes in political regimes (Elias 2007; Flood 2002), in such a way that a consistent universal attitude to this type of representation cannot be concluded.

In addition to necessary considerations of the spiritual context in which the Taxila Buddha statues exist, economic transactions of these artistic objects as they are currently being circulated in Taxila have to be examined. The locally crafted sculptures of the Buddha in Pakistan are part of a commercial market that is implicated in their conception and continuous survival in what could be an ideologically averse milieu. The story of the origins of Buddha sculptures as an art form that has become part of the heritage of Taxila is an oddity. The preservation of this art form through the discovery, revival, and valorization of Buddha sculptures illustrates that heritage can be preserved without any direct interference on the part of institutional actors and influences, and even in spite of it. The historical context in which the Buddha sculptures were incorporated into the heritage assemblage of Taxila informs the complex contemporary state of preservation and the actors involved in it. Around 200 BC, during the time of the Indian emperor, Ashoka, Taxila was known as Taksasila—the "City of Cut Stone." Taksasila developed into an important hub for education, where local Buddhist devotees applied their stone-cutting and carving skills to make the very first anthropomorphic representations of the Buddha (Khan and Hassan 2003). This was the origin of the stone-carving industry.

Modifications in the sculptures produced were a reflection of the history of Taxila and the various rulers that came to govern it. For instance, after the collapse of the Mauryan Empire, the Buddha sculptures produced in Taxila increasingly incorporated various Greek aesthetic influences from the incoming Greco-Bactrian Empire (Dani 1986). This tradition continued until the invasion of the White Huns around 450 AD, when the carvings ceased to be made. It was not until the nineteenth century—when the British administrators of colonial India had Alexander Cunningham carry out archeological excavations, unearthing sculptures from the Gandharan period near the city of Peshawar (Marshall 1951)—that the ancient Gandharan art of Buddha sculpting was revived by the very same stone sculptors in Taxila who had witnessed the resurfacing of this object as part of a coherent archaeological culture. Today, this art form survives in the region's characteristic Gandharan-inspired secular decorative art. Although the Buddhist stone craft industry is flourishing, it does so clandestinely.

The involvement of international agencies charged with the upkeep of Taxila's heritage "authenticity" further obscures the status of Raheem's craft. Since Pakistan's independence in 1947, the federal Archaeology Department has been a steward of preservation for Gandharan art in Pakistan. Pakistan's state-level experimentation with various versions of national identity based on Islam has tended to put these newly formed heritage identities as a Muslim nation in opposition to the ancient pre-Islamic identity of the region. For instance, the pre-Islamic past of the region was sidelined for more "Muslim values" by various governments, and especially military dictatorships such as Zia ul Haq's regime in the 1970s, and this was followed by an ardent policy of Islamization in Pakistan (Devji 2013). Meanwhile, in other areas of Taxila, archaeological sites are still being excavated, producing more evidence of this historical period and its survival in the archaeological record. Some of these discoveries formed the basis for the inclusion of Taxila as a World Heritage Site in 1980 by the United Nations Educational, Scientific, and Cultural Organization (UNESCO). Raheem uses the same criteria to describe the significance of his craft by drawing on UNESCO's rhetoric of a universal significance ascribed to Taxila. However, the emphasis within these criteria on a particular definition of what constitutes authenticity entangles his craft with economic networks of transaction. This entails two types of transactions: Raheem's sculptures are simultaneously considered to be authentic and forged. By UNESCO's standards, the replicas that he produces are not "authentic." However, as they enter a process of becoming forgeries, they are made authentic and fall under the protection of the 1970 Convention. A smuggling mafia is involved in this market, made favorable by the need for sustenance by the artisans who create them. As a result of this complex relationship with contrasting forms of authenticity, the heritage value that has developed around this art form involves diverse forms of "expertise," all of which exclude and even silence the artisans themselves (c.f. De Cesari 2010; Smith 2006). It is in this context that this chapter brings forth the voice of Raheem and other locals engaged in the Gandharan art industry as stone sculptors and artisans, during the summer of 2015.

The Artisans of Taxila

"The Buddha is even mentioned in the Holy Qur'an," explained Raheem upon being asked why he was engaged in the production of these statues, suggesting an immediate understanding of the contradiction that was apparent between his spiritual affiliation and the product of his work. Raheem is a humble and highly respected artisan in the networks of the Buddhist craft and has acquired over 30 years of experience. Simultaneous with his defense of the craft, he clarified, "I think Buddhist art and making such art is completely forbidden according to Islamic law. We cannot even say *but* in this case." But Raheem's paradoxical statements can be better understood in consideration of the context in which the notion of heritage is negotiated in Taxila, through the rhetoric and practices that define heritage locally, and in line with the economic, institutional, and ideological frameworks that inform it.

It is important to point out that the Buddha sculptures in Taxila are neither being used for ritual purposes nor owned by Buddhists within Pakistan, so their heritage value is a negotiation between potential and actual value, not simply as a negotiation that takes place in a pluralistic society but also within the same person. This challenging perspective considers the intricate nuances between diametrically opposed cultural signifiers that are usually presented as binaries, such as the "Muslim versus Hindu" and "Muslim versus Buddhist" dichotomies that are pertinent to the Indian subcontinent. Values attributed to these objects therefore need to be considered in complex shifting contexts—where do the Buddha statues go when they leave Raheem's workshop? They need to reach their designated destination, be that a Buddhist devotee buyer abroad or the mafia network that operates in Taxila. Failing this, they risk exposing Raheem, his craft, and the location where the statues are produced. Raheem must take care not to leave any evidence, such as schist stone lying in front or near his house, which could result in social ostracizing on account of the local mobilization of certain Islamic values, as discussed earlier. He keeps all of his schist stones in his small garden, guarded from the unfavorable context outside.

At first, these locally made replicas were not sold abroad, but a foreign market emerged about 50 years ago when individuals from countries like Japan and South Korea became interested in Gandharan aesthetics. Since Raheem became established as an artisan, however, he has witnessed a decrease in local interest for these sculptures as well as a decline in the amount of foreign sales owing to persisting security issues in Pakistan. Aware that a demand for these sculptures continues to exist abroad, the artists have therefore explored other avenues to reach their customers. Consequently, the way in which these objects move from the workshop to the buyer has undergone enormous transformation. It now involves a mafia network that aids the smuggling of these replicas out of Pakistan—an unlikely steward of preservation for objects that seems to be strategically deployed as both art and heritage, though not to the artisan's advantage. Due to the current economic pressures and a dearth in local buyers, Raheem expressed hesitation at whether he would pass this skill onto his children.

The mafia actors entered the network of production as a response to local legislation and international conventions that hindered the transport of these replicas abroad. Government officials use the 1975 Antiquity Act to harass artisans, and there are reports that state that officials have often attempted to extort money from artisans in return for allowing them to continue making the statues. As a result, Raheem, like others, limits his public exposure. Section 25 of the Act forbids dealing in antiquities unless the artisans obtain a license from the Director General of Archaeology (The Antiquities Act 1975). Over the course of his career, Raheem has tried to obtain this license to export antiquities (available under Form "D" of the 1975 Act) without success. A closer examination of this issue with key stakeholders at the Taxila Museum and the Punjab Small Industries Corporation (PSIC)—a government initiative with the slogan, "Caring for the heritage"—confirmed that in practice this license does not exist. In addition, sections 15–17 of the 1969 Customs Act also prohibit the transport of valuable antiquities (The Customs Act 1969). Despite the fact that Raheem's art is not "antique," these clauses nonetheless affect his work and business model. The smuggling mafia, by virtue of its role as an intermediary in the construction of the statues' value, is a catalyst for the value transformation of statues from "replica" to "antique."[2] According to Raheem, the physical "antique-making process" involves the application of a paste made from mixing liquor together with *chuna* (calcium carbonate) powder and a powder from an older *kanjoos* (black earth from ancient sites), after which the statue is buried underground for a few days for it to acquire the look and feel of an antique. Raheem, now an accomplice in the deceitful collapse of historical authenticity, expressed immense confidence in this technique, claiming that no laboratory in the world could detect the counterfeit. His art, perhaps intrinsically contested in value, assumes extrinsic heritage value far from the privacy of his workshop. However, the sculpture's true value lies in its ability to sustain the artisan. As long as it provides this, Raheem can reconcile the rest.

Like Raheem, Saqib, a fellow sculptor, now works exclusively on commissioned orders. Saqib expressed his intention to leave the craft altogether due to a lack of profit and close his shop, "Gandharan Art," located in the government-funded artisan village at Lok Virsa Museum in Islamabad. This is one of the few initiatives taken by the Pakistani government to make these artists visible. Though they are both sculptors, Saqib and Raheem have selected different business models for their livelihood: While Raheem relies on the smuggling mafia to sell his sculptures, Saqib sells his Buddhist relic caskets in the commercial market. Unlike Raheem, Saqib is able to sell his work on the open market due to the lack of anthropomorphism in the relic caskets. As a result, he is able to strip the caskets of any Buddhist/non-Islamic values as might be perceived by the casual local Muslim shop visitor. He chooses to decorate the relic caskets with floral patterns of the lotus flower, which is iconic in Buddhism. Another important point is that while Saqib does make Buddha sculptures, he does not sell them in his shop for fear of offending local Muslim visitors. He has a table in his shop where he works on the relic caskets. He does this openly without any fear of offending locals, because as long as he is not making anthropomorphic representations, he can publicly engage in this craft. Interestingly, he also makes Islamic art using Gandharan stone, such as decorative tiles with Islamic calligraphy. This is perhaps one of the ways in which he can subvert any conflict in values and continue practicing his craft via appropriation of icons and symbols that are relevant to (and at the same time placate) the Muslim public sphere in which he operates.

Conflicts over the heritage values bestowed upon these art forms are also exacerbated through institutional practices. A conversation with Farooq Ali, Managing Director of PSIC, revealed a specific PSIC initiative for the revival of Taxila stone art. Interestingly, he confessed that during initial planning he had made it clear that they would not "deal with this side [Buddhist art] of Taxila sculptures because of the complexities." This can be understood as a subtle move to encourage artisans to consider creating more marketable items. Instead, PSIC is mainly focusing on developing tiles and other utensils for use in the garden or as materials for construction. But one has to wonder what other institutional mechanisms or lack thereof allow the craft to flourish or perish. Widespread, institutionalized corruption in local governments—largely considered a result of the recent devolution of administrative responsibilities from federal to provincial levels—further obscures the role of institutional machineries responsible for the preservation of heritage in Taxila (Gould et al. 2013). The expectation that this creates, from the perspective of artisans such as Raheem, is that the instruments of government are working intentionally against their work. The ambiguity surrounding the question of whether this craft is legal or not itself complements the ancillary systematic corruption that allows for the mafia to smuggle artifacts out of the country. This also perhaps refocuses the tensions surrounding the Buddha statues of Taxila away from more familiar public debates over the relative place of non-Muslim representational art in Taxila's heritage assemblages.

Discussion and Conclusion

Given his engagement with the black market for antiques and its inherent dangers, Raheem keeps to himself. However, and perhaps surprisingly, he remains undeterred, deferring to the blessings of God as the instrument that helps him overcome all the perils of his craft. Returning to the question that motivated this research, one of the expressed justifications for participating in this craft that recurred in various conversations with Taxila artisans was the recognition of Buddha as a saint. By citing a contested reference about the Buddha in the Qur'an,[3] they dilute any dissonance of their work, as the Buddha is justified by the verse: "No community but that a warner (prophet) has passed in it" (Qur'an: 35:24). Some, of course, reject this view based on the argument that Buddhists are not part of *Ahl al-Kitab* (People of The Book; Tabrizi 2012). Nonetheless, the uncertainty provoked by the appeal to this Qur'anic verse is instrumental in two ways. First, as long as there is ambiguity over the Buddha's status in Islam, the production of Buddhist sculptures can evade socioreligious censure in a context where other representational art—such as Hindu iconographic art—is rarely tolerated. Second, the artisans deploy a carefully crafted discourse to navigate the traditions of Islam and Buddhism strategically. Saqib justified his participation in the craft precisely in this manner, explaining, "If you look at the character of the Buddha, he was a saint like our saints and should be revered instead of being shunned." Such a rhetorical strategy is used by the artisans to nullify any internal conflict involved in crafting idols while remaining followers of Islam. Ultimately, these sets of verbal justifications also aid the artisans as they parse through other ideologically tumultuous terrains.

For instance, at the time of fieldwork, Raheem was working on replicating a Greco-Bactrian plate depicting a homosexual act. While explaining the narrative of this plate, Raheem acknowledged, "Muslims do not believe in this and some even shun it." He then added, "We have no interest in the story; our job is just limited to the scope of art and to just carve out the story from stone." There is a similar method of ideological regulation in operation extending beyond the private toward the public ideological practices of Taxila artisans. Raheem explained that religious locals taunt and threaten him to stop creating sculptures of the Buddha, but he responds, "If I am doing the sin, why are you bothered? And if there is any sin in this [making sculptures], then I will be held responsible not you. But also remember that the One [God] above is so great and forgiving that there are no limits for that. I am just working through His favor and He is helping me throughout." Not only does Raheem evince an internal logic to his practice but also a hierarchy of ideological nominal structures that can be employed with flexibility according to social context. The rhetoric the artisans use in the privacy of their artistic engagements deploys the Buddha's appearance in the Qur'an in order to placate their individual anxieties. However, they remain aware that a mobilization of this association could prove inadequate when faced with the Muslim public sphere. In this context, the artisans do not frame the sculpture as the entity of concern, but rather, their craft. They equate the abstract principles of the craft with the elusive nature of the Islamic God (see also discussions in George 2010).

In conclusion, the conflict concerning the Buddha sculptures of Taxila is not what it first appears to be. A form of conflict between the artisan's private practice and the public sphere is both inevitable and necessary for the continued existence of the Taxila sculptures. This chapter has suggested that what is needed in order to characterize Taxila's heritage is a more nuanced understanding of the economic, institutional, and ideological practices of those involved in the construction of this art form embedded with heritage value. In proposing this, we seek to problematize the idea that heritage value can simply be bestowed on suitable objects through the examination of local agency, independently of global "patterns of exclusion and symbolic meanings" attached to heritage constructs (Bianchi and Boniface 2002). Rather than addressing the relative merit of "pluralism," this type of enquiry places the emphasis and exercise of hierarchy making on non-institutional actors, and considers the negligence and complicity of the state in the construction and the failure of preservation efforts throughout.

Notes

1. Due to the ambiguous and contested public perception of the work of Taxila, we have chosen to anonymize the real names and locations of the artisans throughout this chapter.
2. For more information on intermediary traders and antique runners see, for instance, Jerome Levi, "Commoditizing the Vessels of Identity: Transnational Trade and the Reconstruction of Rarámuri Ethnicity" and Christopher Steiner, "African Art in Transit."
3. The contested reference is usually sourced in the identification of the Prophet Dhu'l Kifl (Al Anbiya 85 and Sad 48).

Bibliography

1969. "The Customs Act 1969." Karachi Chamber of Commerce and Industry Accessed June 15, 2016. https://kcci.com.pk/Rnd/Tax%20Docs/Pakistan%20Customs%20Act%201969,%20updated%2030%20June%202015.pdf.

1975. "The Antiquities Act 1975." International Union for Conservation of Nature (IUCN) Accessed June 15, 2016. http://cmsdata.iucn.org/down loads/antiquities_act_1975.pdf.

Bianchi, Raoul, and Priscilla Boniface 2002. "Editorial: The Politics of World Heritage." *International Journal of Heritage Studies* no. 8 (2): 79–80.

Dani, A. H. 1986. *The Historic City of Taxila*. Tokyo: Centre for East Asian Cultural Studies.

De Cesari, Chiara. 2010. "World Heritage and Mosaic Universalism: A View from Palestine." *Journal of Social Archaeology* no. 10 (3): 299–324.

De Glopper, Charlotte. 2014. "Review of The Politics of Iconoclasm: Religion, Violence and the Culture of Image-Breaking in Christianity and Islam." *Politics, Religion and Ideology* no. 15 (3): 479–480.

Devji, F. 2013. *Muslim Zion: Pakistan as a Political Idea*. Routledge.

Dupree, Nancy Hatch. 2002. "Cultural Heritage and National Identity in Afghanistan." *Third World Quarterly* no. 23 (5): 977–989.

Elias, Jamal J. 2007. "(Un)making Idolatry: From Mecca to Bamiyan." *Future Anterior: Journal of Historic Preservation, History, Theory, and Criticism* no. 4 (2): 12–29.

Elias, Jamal J. 2012. *Aisha's Cushion: Religious Art, Perception, and Practice in Islam*. Cambridge, MA: Harvard University Press.

Flood, Finbarr B. 2002. "Between Cult and Culture: Bamiyan, Islamic Iconoclasm, and the Museum." *The Art Bulletin* no. 84 (4): 641–659.

Francioni, Francesco, and Federico Lenzerini 2003. "The Destruction of the Buddhas of Bamiyan and International Law." *European Journal of International Law* no. 14 (4): 619–651.

George, Kenneth M. 2010. *Picturing Islam: Art and Ethics in a Muslim Lifeworld*. Malden, MA: Wiley-Blackwell.

Gould, William, Taylor C. Sherman, and Sarah Ansari 2013. "The Flux of the Matter: Loyalty, Corruption and the 'Everyday State' in the Post-Partition Government Services of India and Pakistan." *Past and Present* no. 219 (1): 237–279.

Hussain, Zahid. 2015. "Destruction of the Past." DAWN Accessed May 25, 2016. http://www.dawn.com/news/1168714.

Kang, Xiaofei. 2009. "Two Temples, Three Religions, and a Tourist Attraction." *Modern China* no. 35 (3): 227–255.

Karlström, Anna. 2005. "Spiritual Materiality: Heritage Preservation in a Buddhist World?" *Journal of Social Archaeology* no. 5 (3): 338–355.

Khaliq, Fazal. 2016. "Abandoned Heritage: In Jahanabad, World's Biggest Buddha Sculpture Awaits Tourists." The Express Tribune Accessed May 15. http://tribune.com.pk/story/349610/abandoned-heritage-in-jahanabad-worlds-biggest-buddha-sculpture-awaits-tourists/.

Khan, Ashraf, and Mahmood Hassan 2003. "Buddhism and Its Influence on the Cultural Heritage of Pakistan with Special Emphasis on Gandhara." *Journal of Asian Civilizations* no. XXXI (1): 55–59.

Layton, Robert, Peter G. Stone, and Julian Thomas eds. 2001. *Destruction and Conservation of Cultural Property*. London: Routledge.

Levi, Jerome M. 1992. "Commoditizing the Vessels of Identity: Transnational Trade and the Reconstruction of Rarámuri Ethnicity." *Museum Anthropology* no. 16 (3): 7–24.

Levi, Peter. 1972. *The Light Garden of the Angel King: Journeys in Afghanistan*. London: HarperCollins Publishers.

Mani, V.S. 2001. "Bamiyan Buddhas and International Law." The Hindu: Online Edition of India's National Newspaper Accessed 21 May. http://www.thehindu.com/2001/03/06/stories/05062523.htm.

Marshall, John. 1951. *Taxila: An Illustrated Account of Archaeological Excavations Carried Out at Taxila Under the Orders of the Government of India Between the Years 1913 and 1934*. Cambridge: England University Press.

Nagaoka, Masanori. 2011. "Buffering Borobudur for Socio-economic Development: An Approach Away from European Values-Based Heritage Management." *Journal of Cultural Heritage Management and Sustainable Development* no. 5 (2): 130–150.

Noyes, James. 2013. *The Politics of Iconoclasm: Religion, Violence, and the Culture of Image-Breaking in Christianity and Islam*. New York: I.B. Tauris.

Reza, Said. 2012. "Destruction of Bamiyan Buddhas: Taliban Iconoclasm and Hazara Response." *Himalayan and Central Asian Studies* no. 16 (2): 15–50.

Rico, Trinidad. 2016. *Constructing Destruction: Heritage Narratives in the Tsunami City*. London: Routledge.

Rose, Mark. 2007. "Pakistan's Heritage at Risk." Archaeology—A Publication of the Archaeological Institute of America Accessed May 25, 2016. http://archive.archaeology.org/online/features/pakistan/.

Smith, Laurajane. 2006. *Uses of Heritage*. London and New York: Routledge.

Stone, Peter G., and Joanne Farchakh Bajjaly eds. 2008. *The Destruction of Cultural Heritage in Iraq*. Woodbridge, Suffolk, UK: The Boydell Press.

Tabrizi, Taymaz G. 2012. "Ritual Purity and Buddhists in Modern Twelver Shi'a Exegesis and Law." *Journal of Shi'a Islamic Studies* no. 5 (4): 455–471.

Van Der Valk, Arnold. 2014. "Preservation and Development: The Cultural Landscape and Heritage Paradox in the Netherlands." *Landscape Research* no. 39 (2): 158–173.

Zaeef, Abdul Salam. 2011. *My Life with the Taliban*. 1 ed. London: Hurst.

Hassan Asif is a consultant for UNESCO Pakistan. He earned his MA in Museum and Gallery Practice at UCL Qatar and currently conducts research on the role of UNESCO as mediator of different cultural and spiritual values in contemporary and historical heritage projects in Pakistan.

Trinidad Rico is assistant professor and director of the Cultural Heritage and Preservation Studies program at Rutgers University, USA. Her work focuses on ethnographic heritage studies, risk and disaster, cosmopolitanism, and expertise with particular emphasis on the broader Muslim world. She is founding editor of the Pivot series *Heritage Studies in the Muslim World* (Palgrave Macmillan).

Open Access This book is licensed under the terms of the Creative Commons Attribution 4.0 International License (http://creativecommons.org/licenses/by/4.0/), which permits use, sharing, adaptation, distribution and reproduction in any medium or format, as long as you give appropriate credit to the original author(s) and the source, provide a link to the Creative Commons license and indicate if changes were made.

The images or other third party material in this chapter are included in the chapter's Creative Commons license, unless indicated otherwise in a credit line to the material. If material is not included in the chapter's Creative Commons license and your intended use is not permitted by statutory regulation or exceeds the permitted use, you will need to obtain permission directly from the copyright holder.

Index

A
Abbasid period, 32, 99
Abdul-Aziz, king, 71, 75
Abdulhamid II, sultan, 82
Adam's Peak, Sri Lanka, 29
Aga Khan Symposia, 49, 50, 60
Al-A'raf, verse fifty-four, 72–73
Al-jahiliyyah, etymology, meanings of, and use of term, 73–74
Al-Ula museum, Saudi Arabia, 70–71
Al-Ula railway station, Saudi Arabia, 77, 80
'Antique-making,', 117
Antiquities Act (1975), 117
Arabic Kufic inscriptions, Qusayr' Amra, Jordan, 93, 94
Arab ode poetry (*qasida*), 98
Archaeological excavations, 37, 114
Archaeology of Islam, 68, 76, 83
Architecture
　Hijaz Railway as inspiration for revivalist trend in Saudi Arabia, 82
　Islamic, 58, 60, 68, 98
　of museums in Saudi Arabia, 70–71
　symposia, 48
　and transmission of Islamic heritage, 48, 50–51
　vernacular-style mosques in South Asia, 34–35
　Western construct of 'Islamic' tradition in arts and, 96
Artifacts, pre-Islamic, 27–28, 35
Artifacts from Prophet's Mosque (al-Masjid al-Nabawi), 76
Ashoka, emperor, 114
ATBAT-Afrique settlements, 54
Authenticity, heritage and, 5, 59, 92, 114–115

B
Bamiyan Buddhas, destruction by Afghan Taliban (2001), 37, 112, 113
Bani Sakhr Bedouin tribe, 102
Basmala inscriptions, at Qusayr' Amra, Jordan, 93, 95, 101, 104n5
Bhadresvar, Gujarat, 34
Boccaccio, 32
Borobudur Mountain, 33, 37, 40n19
Buddha images
　ambiguity over status in Islam, 119
　in Candi Mendut temple, 33
　destruction of, 37, 112, 113
　Gandharan, 35, 110, 114–115

Buddha sculptures of Taxila,
Pakistan, 110, *111*, 114,
116, 120
Buddhist relic caskets, *111*, 118

C
Caliphs of Abbasid period,
henotheistic position adopted
by, 98
Camel caravans, role in the hajj, 75
Candi Mendut temple, 33
Carrières Centrales, 54
Casablanca, French Morocco,
51–54
Colonialism, and need for Islamic
identity and culture, 48,
51–54
Conservation, 6, 92, 94–95
Critical heritage studies, 2, 83
Cultural appropriations, 97
Cultural continuity, designing
for, 54–58
Cultural differentiation in Islamic
societies, 48
Cultural heritage, Islamic cities as
living emplacement of, 60
Customs Act (1969), 117

D
Dalal (going astray), 68
DAZ Architects, Planners, and
Engineers, 55
Desert castles, Umayyad period, 92
Design process as dialogic
relationship between present and
past, 60–61
Dezful, Iran, 57
Dionysian references in paintings of
Qusayr' Amra, 98, *99*
Disciplinary modes of seeing, 3

E
Egypt, 24–26, 30
European imperialism, 31

F
Faculty of Heritage and Tourism,
Hashemite University, Zarqa, 102
Figurative/representational art
in heritage practices of
Taxila, 112–115, 120
in Islamic heritage, 102
medieval Islamic attitudes
toward, 113
proscription of, in Islamic
devotional settings, 28
at Qusayr' Amra, Jordan, 92–93
in Umayyed period, 92
Fitra concept, 68, 71
French architects in Morocco, 52–53
French Morocco, 53
French North Africa, economic
expansion following World
War II, 53
Friday mosque, Isfahan, Iran, 18, 20

G
Gandharan art and aesthetics, 7,
114, 116
Gandharan stone, 118
Gharbzadegi (Westoxication), 48
Ghaznavid expansion, South Asia, 34
Globalization, disruptions of, 51, 60
Globalization and heritage, 58–59

H
Habitat, conception of, 49–51, 53–55,
58, 60
Hajj route, 68, 75
Hegra (al-Hijr), settlement of, 69

Hellenistic culture in Arabian
  Peninsula, 37
Heritage
  appreciation-creation
    relationship, 20
  as contemporary product shaped
    from history, 3
  globalization and, 58–59
  intersection with concepts of
    Islam, 2, 20, 28
  preservation of, in Diba's design for
    Shushtar No'w, 57
  values of, 112–113, 115–116,
    118, 120
Hijaz Expedition (1917), 80
Hijaz Railway
  aims of examination of, 70
  dichotomies in views of Saudi and
    Turkish scholars, 77
  as inspiration for revivalist trend in
    Saudi architecture, 82
  material remains of, utilized by local
    population, 79–80
  Ottoman Empire and, 75–76
  stations of, as touristic and cultural
    asset of Kingdom, 80
  as symbol of otherness and
    oppression, 78
Hindu Right in India, rejection of
  'pollution' by foreign invasions of
  Persian and Turkish Muslims, 35
Hindu temple ruins, Java, 30, 33–34
Historical perspective on heritage, 5
Housing
  centrally-planned, in Iran, 54–55
  French-designed, based upon
    secular customs in French
    Morocco, 53–54
  Islamic, 48–50, 51–54, 59
  model projects and 'habitat'
    paradigm, 6, 55
Hussayni, Karim Shah, prince, 48–49

I
Ibn Abd al-Barr, 69
Ibn Abd al-Wahhab, Muhammad, 68,
  69–70
Ibn Battuta, 29
Ibn Khaldun, 26
Ibn Nadim, 29
Ibn Taymiyya, 69
Idolatry, and heritage
  preservation, 113
Ilkhanid period, 19
India, 34, 36
Indian Muslim vernacular
  traditions, 35
Indonesia, Muslim response to
  symbols of pre-Islamic pasts, 37
Information boards in exhibition halls
  of Tabuk and Mada'in railway
  stations, 81–82
International Criminal Court in The
  Hague, 37
Iran, 13, 18, 50, 54–55
  See also Shushtar No'w (New
    Shushtar), Iran
Isfahan, Iran, 18–20
Islam
  Ahmed's vision of, as idiom, 29
  conceptual intersection of heritage
    and, 2
  history of origins as contested
    field, 15
  multiple pasts of, 15–17
  as pluriform, 18
  proposed inclusion of stories of
    contestations in history of, 17
Islamic
  art, 7–8, 96
  cities, 48, 59–60
  civilization, expansion across Africa
    and Asia, 29–32
  discourses, diversity of meanings
    in, 20

Islamic (cont.)
  doctrine in Java, 32
  habitat, 49–52, 59–60
  history, 15, 31
  identity and culture, 48–50, 51–54
  nationalism, undermining of political secularism and rise of, 51
Islamic State, destruction of medieval Muslim monuments, 37
Islamization, in Pakistan, 115
Isra'iliyyat, 31

J
Jahanabad Buddha, defacement by Pakistani Taliban, 112
Java, 27, 28, 30
Jewish quarter, Casablanca, 52
Jonah, prophet, in mural paintings of Qusayr' Amra, 95, 97
Jordan, 77
  See also Qusayr' Amra, Jordan

K
Khan Babar village, 110
King Abdul-Aziz Historical Center, Riyadh, Saudi Arabia, 71

L
Le Corbusier, 53
Literary works of antiquity, Boccaccio on, 32

M
Mada'in, Saleh, 13, 15, 69, 81
Madih (panegyrics), 98
Madrid Archaeological Museum, 94
Malabar mosque, Java, 27–28

Maldives, 37
Mamluk campaign of Sultan Selim I, 77
Maritime trade routes, and encounters with material culture of diverse civilizations, 29
Material culture, 15, 29, 68, 77, 83, 113
Mecca, 26, 72, 76, 94, 99
Mediterranean Hellenism, Arab engagements with pre-Islamic culture of, 37
Model housing projects, Iran, 55
Modern heritage process, defined, 61
Mosques, 18, 27–28, 34–35, 75
Muhammad, prophet, 14–15, 96
Mural paintings, see Qusayr' Amra, Jordan
Museums, 37, 70–75, 81, 83, 94
Muslim
  cities, traditional, 49
  culture, medieval, compared to European Renaissance, 32
  engagements with pre-Islamic pasts, 31, 37, 83
  scholarship, concepts of *fitra*, *qadar*, and *dalal* in, 68–69
  societies, contemporary, 103
  travelers, 24–26, 33
Muslim quarter, Casablanca, 52

N
Narrative traditions, 16, 31–38, 72–73
National Museum, Riyadh, Saudi Arabia, 70–75
1970 Convention, 115

O
Ottoman Empire
  exhibition and revival of, 81–82
  and Hijaz Railway, 75–76

National Museum's treatment of, 74
re-purposing of, 77–79
revolt against, 76
utilizing and refurbishing, 79–81

P

Pagan survivals, 30, 36
Pharaonic Egypt, 24–26
Poetry recital competition, "*Al-Jahiliyyah* Era" hall, National Museum, 73
Pre-Islamic culture
  Arab engagements with Mediterranean Hellenism, 37
  artifacts of, 35
  contributions to development of traditions of vernacular Muslim expression, 34
  lack of single normative "Islamic" approach to heritage of, 5
  literature and learning in medieval Persia, 32
  Muslim engagements with, 28–29, 31
Pre-Islamic heritage, rejection of, in language of purification, 36
Pre-Islamic monuments, 24–26, 33–34, 37
Primordial status of Islam, theological questions on, 67–68
Primordial time, 69–70
Prophet's Mosque (al-Masjid al-Nabawi), 76
Punjab Small Industries Corporation (PSIC), 117
Purification, 5, 35–37

Q

Qadar (pre-destination), 68
Qasida (Arab ode poetry/praise hymns), 98

Qur'an
  Buddha's appearance in, and rhetoric of Taxila stone artisans, 115, 120
  history curation in Saudi Arabia and, 70
  role in historical narratives of National Museum, 72–73
  story of Moses's confrontation with Pharoah, 25
  story of Yusuf (Joseph), *sura* twelve, 24–25
  trope of travelling through the land to, see ruins of past-civilizations, 23–24
  use of *isra'iliyyat* in interpretation of, 31
Qusayr' Amra, Jordan
  Arab engagements with pre-Islamic culture of Mediterranean Hellenism, 37
  Bedouin community's understanding of site, 102–103
  conservation interventions, 6, 92, 94–95, 95
  Dionysian references in paintings of, 98
  inscriptions at, 94, 95, 98, 101, 104n5
  mural paintings, 92
  non-Islamic elements in paintings, 96
  painting of 'six kings', 99, 99–101
  qasida 'panel' structure as structure for paintings, 98
  references to Adam, Abraham, and David in mural paintings of, 99
  representation of Prophet Jonah, 96–97, 97
  site management plan, 102–103

Qusayr' Amra, Jordan (*cont.*)
  as UNESCO World Heritage site, 92
Quwwat al-Islam mosque, Delhi, 27

R
Religious appraisal of heritage, 3–4
Rock art, in Hijaz region, 77–79

S
Safavid period, 19
Sasanian period, 13–14, 101
Saudi Arabia
  archaeological work at pre-Islamic sites, 37
  'Islamic' identifier and, 6
  museums, 70–75
  national emblem of Kingdom of, 78–79
  takfirist approach to historiography, 74, 83
  wusum (tribal brands), 78
Saudi Commission for Tourism and National Heritage (SCTH), 71, 73–74, 77, 79–81
Schist stone near gate of Raheem's house, *111*
Scripturalist approaches to 'religion,', 31
SCTH (Saudi Commission for Tourism and National Heritage), 71, 73–74, 77, 79–81
Selim I, Sultan, 77
Seljuk period, 19
Sense of place, construction of, 50
Serat Cabolek, 32
Serat Centhini, 33
Shushtar No'w (New Shushtar), Iran
  Diba's design for, 50, 54–58
  didactic role of, 59
  intentions for, as model community, 6
  pedestrian walkway, 56
  rooftops, 58
  urban configuration of, 56–57
Smuggling mafia, Taxila, Pakistan, 115–119
Somnath, destruction of temple at, 35
South Asia, 34–35
Sri Lanka, 29
Sunan Bonang shrine, Tuban (East Java), 27
Sunni Islam, 98
Surat al-Rum, verse nine, 71

T
Tabuk Archaeology Museum, 81
Tabuk railway station, 77–79, 81
Tahmasp, Shah, 19
Taksasila (City of Cut Stone) [Taxila], 114
Taxila, Pakistan, 109–110, 112–115, 118, 120
Tayma museum, Saudi Arabia, 70–71
Textual production pertaining to Islam, 5, 15, 20
Timurid period, 19
Traditions, invented, 58
Treasures of the past, 26–30

U
Umayyad period, 92–93, 100–102
Umm al-Resas, 38
umma (unity of world Muslims), 48
UNESCO World Heritage sites, 18, 20, 81, 92, 115

United Nations Educational, Scientific, and Cultural Organization (UNESCO), 18, 20, 81, 92, 115

V
Villages, traditional, globalization and disruption of rhythms of, 51
Visual appraisal of heritage, 4

W
Wadi Rum, Jordan, 77
Walid b. Yazid, prince, 92–94, 101, 103, 104–105
Wali Songo grave complexes, 27
WHO (World Heritage Organization), 49
Wusum (tribal brands), northern Saudi Arabia, 78

The manufacturer's authorised representative in the EU is Springer Nature Customer Service Centre GmbH, Europaplatz 3, 69115 Heidelberg, Germany. If you have any concerns regarding our products, please contact ProductSafety@springernature.com

Printed and bound by CPI Group (UK) Ltd, Croydon, CR0 4YY
26/03/2026
02078836-0001